William Netstraeter

A Life in Three Parts

DANIEL JOLLS
&
MICHAEL JOLLS

Praise for

THE FILMS OF
STEVEN SPIELBERG
BY MICHAEL JOLLS

"The book examines in great detail the filmography of one of the most prolific filmmakers that has ever lived."

- **Adam C. Better,** *Amblin Road*

"Tells the story of a shattered childhood relentlessly paved with cinematic triumphs."

- **Sardonic,** *@Sardonica*

"*The Films of Steven Spielberg* is packed so full of information in such a quick read, that unlike *Jaws*, you won't need a bigger boat… or a longer book."

- **Kris Galvan,** *@parkedinfrontofthescreen*

"Michael Jolls really displays his love for film, as well as his love for the great and unforgettable directors that we've had over the years, as he takes us on a journey through Steven Spielberg's tragic childhood, all the way to his rise to the legendary filmmaker we know today, as well as make the reader gain even more of an appreciation for Steven Spielberg's genius films."

- *2 Awesome Men,* **YouTube Channel**

"Highly recommended for film buffs, students and those who are just fascinated by a man that shaped cinema."

- **Luke Andrews,** *The Movie Diorama*

"A fantastic and interesting read!"

- **Alex Fernandes,** *@Movie_Geek98*

Praise for

MAKE HOLLYWOOD GREAT AGAIN

By Michael Jolls

"A smart and in-depth analysis of cinema in the modern political age, demonstrating the extent of Jolls' passion for, and understanding of, cinema as a vehicle for politics."

- **Kate Taylor, *@katereviewsfilms***

"If there was ever a manuscript which needed to be adhered to when creating films with thoughtful principles, *Make Hollywood Great Again* is most definitely one."

- **Sach Harshan, *@TheFilmsCritic***

"A riveting, eyes wide shut account of the political influences on the modern film industry."

- ***@TheNoShitMovieCritic***

"Very insightful read. I couldn't put the book down! Brilliant job by Michael Jolls."

- **Anna Brigitta, *@conservativegirly***

"A fascinating, well-researched, and balanced examination of the ever-evolving relationship between the rhetoric of modern cinema and modern politics."

- **Will Jones, *@film_fanatic44***

Rev. William Netstraeter
— A Life in Three Parts —

By Daniel Jolls & Michael Jolls

Copyright © 2019 Daniel Jolls & Michael Jolls

ISBN-13: 9781696784153

Table of Contents

Introduction..11
Timeline..19

Part I

One - Saint Joseph and the Flight into Egypt..............33
Two - The German Immigrants...................................39
Three - The Succession of Pastors............................57

Part II

Preface to Part II..73
Four - A Bargain..77
Five - Renovation..87
Six - Boomtown...105
Seven - The Politician...119
Eight - Dry vs. Wet..129
Nine – An Era Ends & Another Begins....................141

Part III

Ten – Catholicism vs. National Socialism..................153
Eleven – A Battle of Words....................................173
Twelve – "Put the Money into Brick".......................187
Epilogue..201

Acknowledgements...213
List of Photographs 223
Endnotes..227
Index 235

Introduction

By Michael Jolls:

In early September 2009, Monsignor John Pollard, then pastor of St. Joseph's Catholic Church in Wilmette, asked me to go through the parish memorial books and the sacramental registers to assemble a list of *all* priests who had been appointed to the parish. It was a relatively simple, yet tedious task.

Why? September is the month that St. Joseph's celebrates their annual Oktoberfest, in reference to the parish's German heritage. A few months previous, Pope Benedict XVI designated the summer of 2009 to the summer of 2010 a "year of priests," and this was Monsignor Pollard's way of highlighting both the parish's German heritage and priests.

As I began going through the books and reading the history of St. Joseph's (for the first time), I was awestruck by the story of one pastor with a bizarre last name. Apparently this priest was influential in starting up the popular New Trier High School, was a pseudo real estate developer and was elected mayor of Wilmette…twice?! And, umm, why is Hitler's name popping up in these books?

Let me put this into perspective: I had attended St. Joseph's school for fourth and fifth grade. My family had friends in the parish. I had been working part-time in the office for over a year. Basically, I had some familiarity with the place. But this Father Nessser? Neterator? However you pronounced his name – how did this priest accomplish *so* much and I'm only just reading about him now? I hardly recognized his picture. Unlike the other former pastors, he was neither talked about, nor did he have a room named after him.

I won't forget expressing my shock to Monsignor Pollard and his agreeing with me that the lack of attention given to this priest was an oversight. In fact, we both decided that in anticipation of Oktoberfest, we should place this priest (who's name I kept mispronouncing) on the cover of the weekly bulletin.

Jump to February 2012. I was no longer working at St. Joseph's and was pursuing filmmaking, producing screwball comedies that were getting a little recognition. My endeavors had come to the attention of John Henik, a parishioner from St. Joseph's who asked me to do a Advent/Christmas video. Now, two months later, John was interested in more videos... a lot more.

John was leading the parish's Evangelization Committee with the goal of producing media that would inspire and build interest in the parish. The task of producing a dozen or so videos highlighting different aspects of the parish's activities and organizations didn't seem cost effective, and they would quickly become outdated and need replacing.

An opportunity to correct an oversight presented itself. The magnificent history about the parish and that seemingly forgotten pastor would both inspire and bring newfound interest. One year later, working alongside the same team that I had been making comedies with, we finished *Cathedral of the North Shore*, a documentary that centered on the biography of Father William Netstraeter.

Regardless if you're Catho... hold on, let's clarify something... it's pronounced: "Net-straight-er."

Regardless if you're Catholic or not, regardless if you're religious or not, regardless if you're familiar with Chicago, regardless if you believe in God – Fr. Netstraeter perfectly embodies the American dream and his story remains one that anyone can find inspiring. He was an immigrant to the United States in the post-Civil War era who made the most of a bad situation and helped create a community that still thrives today.

Nancy Canafax, one of the original Fr. Netstraeter enthusiasts (and herself a former president of Wilmette), had been a driving force in keeping his memory alive long before we had the opportunity to make a documentary. When we finished *Cathedral of the North Shore*, there was nothing in the Village of Wilmette or St. Joseph's that truly recognized Fr. Netstraeter's incredible contributions and influence. Within six years after the completion of the documentary, Nancy saw it through to ensure that Fr. Netstraeter's image was embedded on a bronze plaque that now hangs in the entrance of New Trier Township High School. Nancy took the initiative to see that St. Joseph's was recognized with a Sesquicentennial Award by the Illinois Historical Society honoring the longevity of the Parish's service to the state. These efforts snowballed into other results: prior to 2013, Fr. Netstraeter's name didn't even appear on the Wikipedia entry for Cardinal Mundelein's famous paperhanger speech about Adolf Hitler. In the process of doing this book, a simple Google search yield *three times* the number of articles and references to Fr. Netstraeter than there were in 2012 and 2013.

Through Nancy's enthusiasm, I casually began to review the material again, and saw a *new version* of Fr. Netstraeter's story. By no means should that suggest that this book is a different history; rather my research in 2012 was to make a documentary – I wasn't thinking a long form narrative book at the time. A lot gets edited out in filmmaking, hence the term "left on the cutting room floor." Telling Fr. Netstraeter's complete biography in a book allows us to articulate aspects of the history in a format that would not translate cinematically.

Luckily I had copies of everything squirreled away, so all of the research material was still at my disposal. Additionally, I knew where other historical records were kept (i.e. hidden) in St. Joseph's rectory, so I was able to consult those as well.

After recompiling all the material, I took the original narration script used for the film and went to touch it up. I am not exaggerating when I say that my attempt to write two sentences about the relevance of Joseph of Nazareth to the German immigrants turned into a three-hour-long endeavor. I needed help.

By Daniel Jolls:

In the mid-2010s, the Archdiocese of Chicago began merging Catholic parishes all across the Chicagoland area and there was a concern that historical records would be misplaced. It was not until after agreeing to "help" (yeah, right) with this book did I realize *how evident* this concern was. Trying to uncover details from merged parishes was a lost cause. For the sake of history, we had to make sure that Fr. Netstraeter's story, not to mention St. Joseph's parish history, was preserved by way of this book.

Considering that our story begins in the pre-Civil War era and ends at the conclusion of World War II, we needed to break apart these very different settings. This is why *Rev. William Netstraeter* is separated into three distinct parts.

We begin in **Part I** with the rugged northern Chicago territory that the German immigrants settled into in the 1840s. Although Fr. Netstraeter did not arrive until 1867, it is important to commemorate the life of these immigrants and the history of the area to truly understand the environment, community and setting that Fr. Netstraeter would inherit once he arrived.

Fr. Netstreater's life (the subject of **Part II**) would find its way into a blend of professions from religious leader, real estate developer and political influencer. In these areas, Fr. Netstraeter saw success during his lifetime, although the true enigma of his story were the events after this death. On a local level, Fr. Netstaeter's accomplishments would directly impact the layout of the modern north shore of Chicago. His efforts marketing the Village of Wilmette would progressively come to fruition in the following decades, making the town one of the most desired neighborhoods of the Chicagoland area.

On the global stage, Fr. Netstraeter played a posthumous role in a political tête-à-tête between Cardinal George Mundelein and Chancellor Adolf Hitler. **Part III** is devoted to this drama as we explore the backstory of Hitler's artistic ambitions and the brimming uneasiness between the ideologies of the Nazi Party and the Roman Catholic Church throughout the 1930s. By the end, hopefully you will see the contrast between the Nazis and Fr. Netstraeter — one extracted and exiled Germans *out* of their homes, where as the other encouraged Germans to build from *within*.

***

This biography is an independent work. We were not asked by St. Joseph's Parish, the Archdiocese of Chicago, a historical society or any one parishioner or person to write this book. *This endeavor was our own.* Although St. Joseph's allowed us to consult the parish archives, the manuscript was never submitted to them for approval. Although we consulted the Archdiocese of Chicago for factual questions, they were not sent a manuscript for approval. The same goes for all the organizations we spoke with in the process of writing this book. We were not asked to put this disclaimer. We are stating this so that the reader knowns that the history presented here is objective.

Finally, we must note that much of the early history wasn't as detailed as we would have liked. However, we were able to come up with accurate explanations when material was lacking. Additionally, we followed up with every organization to uncover any details that were not known. If there is still material out there on Fr. Netstraeter that we were unable to uncover, we hope this book will inspire that material to come forth. With so much assistance, we should have written a perfect book, but, of course, perfection isn't possible. We alone are responsible for all errors.

Timeline

- Part I -

1833 — The federal government purchases 5 million acres from the Native Americans at $0.15 an acre. The majority of the Native Americans leave the area except the Pottawatomie who gather in a village (now present-day Evanston Hospital).

Late 1830s — German immigrants from Trier begin arriving in the Grosse Pointe territory of northern Chicago (present-day north shore area).

January 1, 1843 — William Netstraeter is born to parents Franz Netstraeter & Maria Schulte* in Westphalia, Germany.

February 1843 — German immigrants build a 24 x 30 foot log cabin "church" and name it Saint Joseph's Mission.

November 21, 1845 — Bishop Quarter of the Chicago Diocese formally recognizes the

---

*Contrary to "Maria Schulte", a genealogy account lists Fr. William Netstraeter's mother as "Josephine Frances (Sels)". We believe that "Maria" is the correct name as it appears on both Franz Netstraeter's & William Netstraeter's death certificates.

	St. Joseph mission as a parish. Father Gerhard H. Plathe becomes the first pastor of Saint Joseph's.
October 1847	German-speaking priest Father Johann Fortmann is appointed as the second pastor of St. Joseph's parish.
Early 1849	A larger 30 x 90 foot log cabin church is built replacing the old one. It is believed that Fr. Fortmann worked hand-in-hand with the builders.
April 21, 1850	Dedication of the new St. Joseph's church by Bishop James O. Van de Velde, S.J.
Early 1852	Against parishioners' wishes, the Chicago Diocese removes Fr. Fortmann. His replacement only stays two months before leaving. St. Joseph's "parish" is temporarily reduced to a mission.
Fall 1852 to 1865	St. Joseph's goes through a series of six pastors.
Summer 1865	Fr. Bernard Heskemann visits the parish and instantly becomes enchanted with the growing neighborhood. He offers his services as pastor and is formally appointed on October 15.

1866	Bishop Quarter closes the University of St. Mary of the Lake as it becomes too much of a financial burden.
March 1867	William Netstraeter, a sub-deacon, emigrates from Germany to the United States and begins studies at St. Francis seminary in Wisconsin.
September 29, 1867	William Netstraeter is ordained a priest in Wisconsin.
January 26, 1868	The St. Joseph parishioners decided to build a new church costing $20,000. However, throughout 1868 only $12,000 is collected in pledges.
1869	Sixty-five German Catholics found a secondary "St. Joseph's Mission" 4 miles south (now present-day St. Peter's Parish in Skokie).
1871	St. Joseph's decides to take out loans with an extremely high interest rate that skyrocket the cost of the church's construction. By the following year, the cumulate debt rises to $15,000.

- Part II -

Spring 1872 — With the massive debt and an unattractive ad-hoc roof, Fr. Heskemann has a mental breakdown and leaves St. Joseph's for a cloistered sanctuary in Indiana.

May 1872 — Bishop Thomas Foley offers Fr. Netstraeter the pastor job at St. Joseph's, under the condition that if Fr. Netstraeter can stabilize the parish in two years, he will be given a prestigious parish in the city of Chicago. Upon his arrival, Fr. Netstraeter greets every single home in his new parish.

August 1872 — Members of the community vote to create the Village of Wilmette.

Early 1873 — The roof of the church is fixed.

Summer 1873 — A new frame school house is built.

September 18, 1873 — A banking crisis begins, sparking an economic depression.

1874 — The Village of Gross Point is incorporated. The boundaries between Wilmette and Gross Point lay directly across the street from St. Joseph's church.

	As opposed to "dry" Wilmette and Evanston, the village of Gross Point is authorized to sell alcohol.
1876	A second floor is added to St. Joseph's school to house teachers.
September 1877	Fr. Netstraeter convinces the School Sisters of St. Francis in Milwaukee to come and teach at St. Joseph's school.
1881	The church is renovated and redecorated.
1882	Fr. Netstraeter becomes a trustee on the Wilmette Village Board. One of the reasons for doing so was to politically push Gross Point to become "dry" as the saloons across the street are an embarrassment for St. Joseph's.
1886	After serving four consecutive years as a trustee, Fr. Netstraeter is elected mayor of Wilmette for a one-year term.
	A new rectory is built across the street. The old rectory is converted into a convent for nuns.

1890	Fr. Netstraeter is reelected as village mayor for another one-year term.
Early 1890s	Fr. Netstraeter pushes to have Wilmette annexed to the neighboring city of Evanston. The referendum fails.
1892	Four additional classrooms and an auditorium is added to the school at the back end of the campus.
December 1892	At the encouragement of Fr. Netstraeter, the Franciscan nuns who teach at the school decide to acquire land to construct a water treatment sanitarium two blocks north of St. Joseph's. The following month the Village of Wilmette pushes back and the project falls through, leaving the large plot of land empty. Over the years, Fr. Netstraeter sells off parcels of it. Eventually, the present-day Mallinckrodt Center is built there.
1899	Fr. Netstraeter joins a board that is established to begin the prospects of a new school for higher learning. In December, bonds of $60,000 are issued to begin the new school.

1901	The new school for higher education is completed and is named "New Trier" in honor of the German's home region.
1907	Along with 18 families, Fr. Netstraeter assists with building a new church 4 miles west of St. Joseph's in Glenview. The dedication of this new church takes place on November 1 (now present-day Our Lady of Perpetual Help).
	Fr. Netstraeter steps down from New Trier's school board.
	In Austria, an 18-year-old art student named Adolf Hitler moves to the city of Vienna, but fails in getting into the art and architecture schools of his choice. He spends the next four years doing landscape paintings and menial "art" jobs such as wallpaper hanging.
1909	The Village of Gross Point is out voted to cease the sale of alcohol. The new law crushes Gross Point's economy.
1913	Fr. Netstraeter purchases land in Skokie to assist non-Catholics with having a cemetery (now

	present-day Memorial Park Cemetery).
1921	Archbishop George Mundelein begins plans to re-open St. Mary of the Lake Seminary that Bishop Quarter had closed over 50 years ago.
July, 1923	Fr. Netstraeter retires as pastor of St. Joseph's. Father John A. Neumann replaces him.
April 7, 1924	Fr. Netstraeter dies. His will indicates that his entire estate, a sum of $300,000, be left for St. Joseph's parish, specifically for the construction of a brand new church.

- Part III -

1924	The Village of Gross Point is annexed with majority of the property taken over by the village of Wilmette; smaller portions were annexed to Evanston and Skokie.
1926	Archbishop Mundelein officially re-opens St. Mary of the Lake Seminary. In doing so, he borrows the full sum of Fr. Netstraeter's estate as St.

	Joseph's doesn't have set plans on how to use the gifted money.
July 1934	Adolf Hitler becomes chancellor of Germany. The Nazi party ranks highest in the government.
	Present Franklin D. Roosevelt sends a letter commending Fr. Neumann and St. Joseph's on the construction of a new school building.
1935	An increase in trials of religious leaders takes place throughout Nazi Germany.
1937	In the Upper Bavaria region of Nazi Germany, Catholic schools are replaced with "common schools."
March 10, 1937	Pope Pius XII officially denounces the Nazi regime.
May 18, 1937	Cardinal Mundelein publically denounces Hitler and the members of his inner circle. The Cardinal calls Hitler a "one arm paper hanger" and the nickname catches on, being repeated by those who oppose Hitler.
August 1937	Without any foreknowledge, a lawsuit is suddenly filed from relatives in Nazi Germany

	claiming to be family members of the late Fr. Netstraeter. The family says they are entitled to the will, hence the $300,000, and not the Archdiocese of Chicago, which Cardinal Mundelein operates. Through three separate court hearings, the Archdiocese of Chicago and St. Joseph's are declared the rightful owner of Fr. Netstraeter's will. The Vatican instructs Cardinal Mundelein to instantly begin building the church that the money was intended for.
April 1938	Ground is broken for a brand new St. Joseph's church in Wilmette across the street from the location of the current church.
1939	All Catholic schools in Germany are closed and converted to public facilities.
September 1, 1939	Nazi Germany invades Poland. The country falls within three days. Britain and France declare war on Germany, officially starting World War II.
September 24, 1939	Fr. Netstraeter's final wish comes true as Cardinal Mundelein dedicates the new, massively larger, St. Joseph's church. Unbenownist to all, this

	is to be Cardinal Mundelein's last public appearance.
October 2, 1939	At the age of 67, Cardinal Mundelein unexpectedly dies in his sleep.

- Epilogue -

March 1941	Catholic press is outlawed in Nazi Germany.
December 11, 1941	Less than a week after the Japanese bomb Pearl Harbor, Hitler declares war on the United States. The U.S. joins with the Allied Forces.
June 6, 1944	American troops begin landing in Nazi occupied France.
July 23, 1944	Russian forces discover a work camp near the city of Lubin in Poland that displays evidence of mass murder.
April 1945	Allied forces begin stumbling on and liberating many work camps, revealing drastically high volumes of mass murder.
April 30, 1945	Hitler shoots himself in his private study.

May 8, 1945	The Nazis unconditionally surrender to the Allied Forces, ending Europe's involvement in World War II. By this date over 2,500 Catholics were killed by the Nazis.
1946	The parish census of St. Joseph's is marked at approximately 500 families.
1956	The once little German mission's census tallies approximately 1,200 families, remaining one of the most prominent German establishments in Chicago's north shore.

Part I

Chapter One
Saint Joseph and the Flight into Egypt

Despite that many of the figures discussed in this biography were active members of the Catholic church, this narrative is a work of history and not a religious evangelization. Given this, it may seem odd to privilege a Biblical story for a narrative set in the late 1800s and early 1900s. If you do not believe in the supernatural or are skeptical of material in the Bible, the fact remains that the German immigrants and Fr. Netstraeter *did* believe in the Biblical version of Jesus Christ. This excerpt from Jesus' and Joseph's biography plays a significant role in why the title of "St. Joseph" was used by the German immigrants, as well as why he had prominence in their community.

Hence, our story begins around 4 or 6 A.D.

Joseph of Nazareth

The exact date of Jesus' birth is not known, but we do know that he was born sometime during the Census of Quirinius, when King Herod I was the Rome-appointed leader of Judea. Mandated by the Roman government, this census of the Judea region ordered that any families not living in their city of birth had to temporarily return to their home cities for the count.

Joseph, a carpenter by trade and a newlywed, was living in Nazareth when the census decree was made. As ordered, Joseph and his new wife, Mary, were ordered to travel over 100 miles south to his hometown of Bethlehem. Adding to the difficult journey, Mary was pregnant with their firstborn. Not long after arriving in Bethlehem, Mary gave birth to Jesus.

Within a few days of Jesus' birth, the family was visited by three mystics, believed to have traveled from Persia, Babylonia, and India. These three scholars (also referred to as "three wise men," "magi" or "kings") had followed astronomical signs indicating the birth of the "new king;" specifically the "Messiah." In the Jewish faith, the "Messiah" is prophesied to be the great liberator of the Jewish nation and would lead the Jews to salvation within the world. The Catholic faith believes that Jesus, son of Joseph and Mary, was this "Messiah."

According to the Gospel of Matthew's rendition of the story, Herod was aware that various prophets were predicting the birth of the Messiah, and so he orchestrated a secret meeting with the three traveling mystics. Herod wanted to know the location of the newborn so that he could also pay homage to this "new king." Yet the three mystics were warned in a dream not to return to Herod with the location of Jesus, Mary and Joseph. At the same time, Joseph too was visited by an angel in a dream. According to the Gospel of Matthew, the text reads:

> The angel of the Lord appeared to Joseph in a dream and said, "Rise, take the child and his mother, flee to Egypt, and stay there until I tell you. Herod is going to search for the child to destroy him." Joseph rose and took the child and his mother by night and departed for Egypt. He [Joseph] stayed there until the death of Herod, that what the Lord had said through the prophet might be fulfilled, "Out of Egypt I called my son." [1]

Catholic tradition believes that Herod ordered the execution of all male children, ages two and younger to prevent the birth of a new Jewish king that was assumed to inevitably upend his bloodline. [2] Again, the Gospel of Matthew indicates:

> When Herod realized that he had been deceived by the [three] magi, he became furious. He ordered the massacre of all the boys in Bethlehem and its vicinity two years old and under, in accordance with the time he had ascertained from the magi. [3]

Although some historians have discredited this mass killing of babies as creative fiction on the part of Christian folklore, it functions as an allegorical parallel to Moses, the "deliverer" of the Jewish people.

The correlation between Jesus and Moses is central to the entire Christian faith, as Moses is believed to be a prefigurement of Jesus. Moses was born in Egypt, when Paraoh Seti I was convinced that the Hebrews were growing in numbers so quickly that they could potentially overthrow the Egyptian dynasty or be recruited by Egypt's enemies. Seti ordered that midwives kill all the Hebrew male babies, of which Moses was one of the few survivors. So too, would Jesus survive Herod's attempt to kill him as a infant.

As the birth year of Jesus is not finite, the various timelines suggest different answers to how long Joseph, Mary and Jesus remained in Egypt. We do know that the family remained in Egypt anywhere from a couple of months to two years at most. Nevertheless, in the Christian tradition it is believed that soon after the mass murder of the male-born babies, King Herod was overtaken by an unidentified and very painful illness. Driven by paranoia and physical ailments, Herod stabbed himself to death. In the Gospel of Matthew it reads:

> When Herod had died, behold, the angel of
> the Lord appeared in a dream to Joseph in
> Egypt and said, "Rise, take the child and

his mother and go to the land of Israel, from those who sought the child's life are dead." He [Joseph] rose, took the child and his mother, and went to the land of Israel. (4)

Inspiration for the Germans

There are a couple of items to note from this Biblical story in regards to the story of the early German immigrants in Chicago. First is that Joseph's travels are a source of inspiration for immigrants. As head of the household, Joseph is moving his family from Nazareth, 100 miles south to Bethlehem, then over 350 miles southwest to the foreign Egypt and finally back north, 450 miles to Nazareth. All of this seemingly nomad migration, on foot, is at the direction of God. Joseph is fleeing certain death as he's supposed to have possession of the child that is prophesied to become a grand ruler and overthrow all kingdoms on Earth. In some ways, Joseph is persecuted for his faith — much like the German Catholics in Prussia who migrated to the United States in the 1840s. Additionally, although Joseph's exact birth and death dates are not known, history suggests that he was a widower and an older man when wed to Mary. Although Joseph was of royal lineage, being a descendant of King David, he was neither a wealthy individual nor any sort of community leader. The German Catholics coming to the United States were not members of the high class; rather, they were farmers. These Germans were people who worked the land and sought to pass on the skills of farming to their children, similar to how Joseph passed along the skills of carpentry to Jesus.

Immigrants draw strength from the story of Saint Joseph, particularly the extensive migration he took in the weeks of Mary's pregnancy and birth of Jesus.

Chapter Two
The German Immigrants
(1840 to 1847)

Please note:
In the 1830s, the region of "Grosse Pointe" is in reference to the entire forest territory approximately 14 miles north of Chicago.(1) This area is now the modern-day suburbs of Evanston, Glenview, Kenilworth, Northbrook, Northfield, Skokie, Wilmette and Winnetka.

In this text, when referencing "Grosse Pointe," we are referring to the unsettled wilderness - not the "Village of Gross Point" which did not incorporate until 1874, thirty years later.

In the year 1840, the country of Prussia (now current Germany) was intertwined with wars of unification, leading to circumstances that were oppressive to the Catholics living in the Protestant-controlled country. The German Catholics who left their homes in the regions of Trier, the Rhineland and the Moselle Valley arrived in the northeast coast of the United States. Those who landed in the states of Illinois and Wisconsin traveled both by railroad and the St. Lawrence Seaway; the St. Lawrence River runs between the countries of Canada and the United States, connecting the Atlantic Ocean with the five Great Lakes.

A community of Germans pioneered land 14 miles north of Chicago in a territory referred to as Grosse Pointe. The exact reasons why these German immigrants established a homestead in the Grosse Pointe region is not known, but history offers a few clues that help deduce some explanations:

To begin, these Germans left a country with fertile fields and established communities with (we can safely assume) comfortable homes. They willingly chose to endure the travel of moving from Trier to Chicago - a distance of over 4,300 miles - across an ocean and land into a country with a different language. Ultimately, these Germans resolved to settle in the wilderness and acclimate in a forest that was recently inhabited by Native Americans. Furthermore, there is no indication if the German settlers knew of or even discussed the Grosse Pointe territory as the intended place of living.

It should be noted that the discovery of gold in California (kicking off the Gold Rush) wasn't public knowledge until March or April of 1848 at the earliest. Although there were some instances of Grosse Pointe families having money sent back home from gathering gold out west — the German settlers landed approximately five or six years prior to the announcement of gold. Hence, they were not undertaking the difficult travel from Europe to the United States for the prospect of gold nuggets. Furthermore, based off general observations of the founders of St. Joseph's Parish (circa 1843), there is nothing to suggest that materialism drove them from Germany to the United States.

A log house from the Grosse Pointe territory, built in approximately 1837.

What the older records also suggest is that immigrants were rational men; not refugees or wandering vagrants.(2) There is no documentation suggesting that the immigrants brought an excess of materials for a longer journey westward and decided to cut it short when arriving to the wilderness of northern Illinois. The German immigrants of Grosse Pointe were not explorers; they were settlers digging new roots.

There were also ideological reasons why the German Catholic immigrants of the 1840s chose to leave their fatherland when they did. The Germans immigrating to the United States of America were drawn to the concept of a "free" country, particularly freedom of religion. In America, these Germans were free from a restrictive government (much less a government at war), and could practice their Catholic faith in a country with no state church. Any government that engages in religious persecution will inevitably kill patriotism within the persecuted group. Hence, why would these German Catholics want to remain affiliated with a "fatherland" that treated them poorly?

The more principled reasons why Germans were migrating to the United States was the understanding that in America, these immigrants could purchase and maintain their *own* land. As opposed to Germany, the ownership of land was something exclusive to the wealthier aristocratic class in the 1830s and 1840s. Since farming was their profession and primary economy, the selection of the Grosse Pointe territory made sense. The ground was flat, the soil was rich and was close to a large water source (Lake Michigan).

As for the Native Americans, in 1829 there was a great gathering of the tribes at Prairie du Chien (on the border of Iowa and Wisconsin), where the Natives were offered a treaty for the land by the U.S. government. The Grosse Pointe area was a part of this vast exchange. By the time of the German immigrants' arrival, the majority of the Native Americans had already moved west. Nevertheless, there were still concerning factors to consider: the Black Hawk War (April to August of 1832) had taken place along the western boundaries of Illinois, Iowa and Wisconsin. This bloody conflict increased tensions between settlers and Natives, although a Pottawatomie village in the area (located where present-day Evanston Hospital sits) was a tribe that strived for peace between the two groups. One of the Native's trails, named the Green Bay trail by the settlers, became the primary route in which pioneers began to settle. Hence, the presence of Native Americans was uncommon, although not unusual.

The exact buying and selling of land in the Grosse Pointe area has become very distorted throughout history: for example, the first family that settled and purchased land from the Native Americans, the Ouilmette family from France, began selling off land reservations in 1829 — even though President James K. Polk did not issue his approval until May 14, 1847. By the mid-1840s, there was an estimated 40 landowners in the area.

A photograph of what the Grosse Pointe territory probably looked like when the farmers first arrived.

Nevertheless, the purchasing of large quantities of land would become a very lucrative business over the next twenty years (until the post-Civil War era). Immigrant families purchased large amounts of land ideally for farming, and as time went on, the land was then sold to newcomers at a markup. Like any economy, the numbers fluctuate and certain areas of Grosse Pointe were more desirable than others, but from a historical perspective, the increase in value is obvious. Taking random selections from the records, consider the following:

- In 1835, 640 acres were sold for $1,100 (approx. $1.72 an acre)

- In 1840, 18.78 acres were sold for $23.44 (approx. $1.24 an acre)

- In 1841, 102.98 acres were sold for $128.44 (approx. $1.25 an acre)

- In 1841, 84.54 acres were sold for $105.68 (approx. $1.25 an acre)

- In 1844, 100 acres were sold for $600 (approx. $6.00 an acre)

- In 1851, 270 acres were sold for $1,050 (approx. $3.89 an acre)

- In 1857, 120 acres were sold for $13,173 (approx. $109.78 an acre) [3]

These compounded reasons encouraged the German settlers to willingly participate in the American economic system. As recorded in an early anthology:

> Thus the early [German] settlers of St. Joseph were easily absorbed and readily adopted American institutions. Even their mother tongue surrendered to the American. They became full-fledged, tax-paying Americans. Thrifty truck-farmers, gardeners, home-builders -- the nation's fundamental asset in terms of loyalty and productivity.(4)

An early communal act determined that they constructed a 24 x 30 foot log cabin mission church. The property for this log cabin church was given to the immigrants by Michael Diversey, an early Chicago financier (whom the present-day Diversey Street is named after). The German immigrants are believed to have finished the log cabin in February 1843, and named the mission church after St. Joseph, the carpenter from the Bible.

Despite being a log cabin, one has to understand the significance of a physical "church" or a "house of worship" to the German immigrants from the perspective of the early 1840s. The formation of the St. Joseph's Mission was possible in a "free" country, a country where these immigrants would reinstate their Catholic faith, both through the traditions and a physical building. This expression of religious freedom served the purpose of reinstating their heritage and removing a stigma of persecution.

Prices in Chicago as listed in one of the "Hoffmann Letters" from summer 1845.

Cow	$ 8.00
Yoke of Oxen	$30.00
Horse	$30.00
150 Pound Hog	$ 2.25
200 Pound Hog	$ 4.00
150 Pound Hog	$ 2.25
1 Pound of Beef	$ 0.04
1 Pound of Pork	$ 0.03
1 Pound of Coffee	$ 0.10
200 Pounds of Salt	$ 1.75
200 Pounds of Sugar	$ 0.10
Bushel of Potatoes	$ 0.25
Barrel of Flour	$ 4.00
Cord of Wood	$ 2.00

Labor Wages

Bricklayer	$ 1.25 to $ 1.50 a day
Wagon Maker	$ 0.75 to $ 1.00 a day
Day Laborer	$ 0.50, plus a meal

Dated July 31, 1845, these figures are taken from one of the letters from the Hoffmann's family correspondence to relatives back in Germany.

48 Rev. William Netstraeter

Although these images of various Grosse Pointe farmers were taken in the late 1800s and early 1900s, they are the best visual reflection of the lifesytles during this era. Pictures from the St. Joseph's Parish archives:

The German Immigrants 49

The German Immigrants 51

Recognized as a Parish

On November 28, 1843, Bishop William Quarter was appointed as the first bishop of the Chicago diocese. Sometime after May 1844, Bishop Quarter sent his only German speaking priest(5) to the St. Joseph's mission. At some point within the two year period, another priest(6) was sent, although parish history records are unable to indicate the exact arrival and departure of these priests. These priests' respective relationships with the Germans in Grosse Pointe is foggy at best; there are some indications of sacraments dispensed, yet when correlated to other outposts that the Diocese of Chicago was attempting to establish at the time, the records become obscured. Furthermore, as vital as religion was to the German community, there were other concerns that were more pressing to the early pioneers. The forest in which they chose to settle was pure wilderness, hence the construction of society (i.e. homes, roads, buildings, schools, farms) in anticipation of future generations took priority.

From a parochial perspective, a Diocese can be viewed as a crutch towards the operation of a church, yet for a rugged community in the early years of formation, the recognition of "parish" meant that the sacramental needs of these German settlers would be properly serviced. Additionally, the Diocese of Chicago would assume responsibility for staffing St. Joseph's with a priest and overseeing the church's general maintenance.

***

On November 21, 1845, Bishop Quarter officially recognized St. Joseph's "mission" as a "parish," approximately two years after the completion of the log cabin.* On this same date, a pastor was assigned. Originally from Boston, Rev. G. Herman Plathe (pronounced "Platte")† was appointed as the first pastor, a position intended to be more permanent, in lieu of trying to find priests who would occasionally visit.

Fr. Plathe remained at St. Joseph's for two years, doing the best he could to offer ecclesiastical services to the Germans. Seven months after Fr. Plathe's appointment, 41 children received their first Holy Communion, and 24 teenagers received Confirmation from Bishop Quarter himself on June 21, 1846. The number of children indicates that many families were settling in the Grosse Pointe area. At the same time, St. Joseph's was the only Catholic church in approximately a 15 mile radius (possibly more), which attributes to why Fr. Plathe's priestly functions were not limited to

---

* Since the founding of St. Joseph's is dated 1842, but it was not officially recognized as a "parish" until 1845, there is some debate as to its official age.

† Many of St. Joseph's history albums say Rev. Gerhard M. Plathe. After reviewing his signature on the actual Baptismal register from the 1840s, we discovered that it says "G.H. Plathe". We can safely assume that the "M" was a forgivable misreading of the old and blurry cursive.

the Grosse Pointe farmers in the immediate area. Fr. Plathe's and St. Joseph's pastoral care for Catholics encompassed all of modern-day northern Cook County, Lake County (which stretches up to the Wisconsin border), and all of McHenry County. Although this vast stretch of land — a rectangle of about 70 square miles - was primarily wilderness, this was an outrageously large territory for just one priest and one parish.

Although a train track ran north and south from Chicago to Milwaukee, the primary transportation west bound was by horse or on foot. St. Joseph's log cabin was a half mile (possibly less) from the train line, which made it convenient for fellow Germans to connect with each other, and made St. Joseph's a landmark in the late 1840s.

The sign outside of the current St. Joseph's church depicts the wooden log cabin surrounded by trees on both sides with the year 1843 etched above.

The German Immigrants 55

The Log Cabin Mission
Artwork by Mary Delaney, Parishioner

Concept art found in St. Joseph's archives probably intended for parish related events, publications, Sunday bulletins, etc. The large cross above the log cabin resembles the stone façade that "bookends" the front and back of the current St. Joseph's church.

Chapter Three
The Succession of Pastors
(1847 to 1872)

Father Johann N. Fortmann

In October 1847, Fr. Plathe was transferred down to southern Illinois and Father Johann N. Fortmann was sent to replace him as pastor. From both a historical and ironic perspective, the appointment of Fr. Fortmann was both a great blessing to St. Joseph's and the catalyst for the drama that would encompass the parish for the next two decades. Although Fr. Fortmann remained in the Grosse Pointe area for only five years, the few historical records indicate that his tenure would heavily correlate to the impact Fr. Netstraeter would have 18 years later.

***

In 1847, the Grosse Pointe territory was still very much a "backwoods" area, meaning that the physical construction of a society (the buildings and roads) remained relatively barren when compared to the cities of Chicago 15 miles south, Joliet 60 miles southwest, or Galena 160 miles west. The future towns and governments of Evanston, Gross Point, Skokie, and

Wilmette were still in a formation phase and wouldn't be incorporated for at least a dozen years or so. By no means should this suggest that "culture" was lacking among the inhabitants. On the contrary, those living in Grosse Pointe were intent on creating a permanent home. They sought culture, education and government in an effort to create a homestead for future generations. Fr. Fortmann fit the qualifications; he was German and wanted to participate in the lifestyle of his parishioners.

The records from this era are scarce (some are believed to have been lost in the Great Chicago Fire in 1871),[1] however, given the tidbits and facts about Fr. Fortmann, the circumstances of the Grosse Pointe territory, and the events that followed after Fr. Fortmann's exit, we can safely assume the following narrative is historically accurate:

Fr. Fortmann was exactly ten years ordained a priest when he arrived at St. Joseph's, which suggests that he was likely in his early or mid-30s. Hence, Fr. Fortmann was young but not wholly inexperienced; he had the endurance and stamina to work in a budding community. Fr. Fortmann was also a native of Germany, so there was no language barrier. He participated in the pioneering activities — both which quickly endeared him to his parishioners. Every anthology about the parish highlights that Fr. Fortmann was comfortable with manual labor and was also a carpenter like their patron saint, Joseph.

By 1849, as the settlement(s) grew, the original log cabin church had become inadequate and parishioners decided it should be replaced with a larger, 30 x 90 foot frame log cabin church (probably completed in 1850). Fr. Fortmann was careful with the small funds that St. Joseph's had to see this project through. Some histories have indicated that Fr. Fortmann sweated alongside the workers when constructing the larger log cabin church. However, this could be creative fiction; a different record suggests that Fr. Fortmann was not permitted to participate in manual labor despite his carpentry knowledge.

Based off two fragmented diary notes[2], one gets the impression that Fr. Fortmann made Catholic traditions, rituals and practices an important element of his pastorate. One letter from a German immigrant writing to family back home reads:

> Like our first pastor, he [Fr. Fortmann] came from Münster, Westfalen. He is a true follower of the apostles and a disciple of our Lord. Sunday services consist of High Mass, Latin singing, and old German Hymns.
>
> In the afternoon we have catechism and Vespers. Our church service is very similar to that of which we had in Kessling. [3]

Although history doesn't offer many more details, what we see under Fr. Fortmann's tenure is that there was a steady number of participants in the sacraments and there were more visits from the bishop. Due to the backlash from parishioners following Fr. Fortmann's sudden departure, history suggests that the Germans had incredible fondness for him. The overall notations in the history lead us to presume that Fr. Fortman was a very holy priest.

Immigrants from any country often make an ardent effort to authentically recreate their culture and home in the "new world" of America. Many of the Christian Germans in Grosse Pointe, not just the Catholics, wanted to embed their heritage and tradition into the new society they were building. Grosse Pointe was to be these Germans' home for future generations, hence it's no surprise that they were grateful for a religious figure that could relate to them and encourage dutiful observance of the Christian faith.

Specifically for Catholics, throughout the history of the Roman Rite Church, reverence to the sacred and devoutness to religious practices have proven to remain the best stimulant to the success and growth of the Church. Hence, because Fr. Fortmann maintained a devoutness to religious celebrations, the German Catholics were clearly enthused.

13 Years, 8 Pastors (1852 to 1865)

In circa 1851, after officiating at a Confirmation at St. Joseph's, Bishop James Oliver Van de Velde stopped approximately halfway between St. Joseph's and the city of Chicago to make arrangements for a new parish that would become St. Henry's. Fr. Fortmann was appointed to oversee the construction of St. Henry's church, as well as attend to the spiritual needs of the new parish, consisting primarily of Luxembourgers and Germans.

In May 1852, at the direction of the Diocese of Chicago, Fr. Fortmann was formally transferred from St. Joseph's to St. Henry's. The specific details are lost to history (again, perhaps there were more records that were lost in the Great Chicago Fire), yet the common retelling is that the parishioners of St. Joseph's immensely resented this decision, feeling that they were being neglected in favor of newer parishes.

To better understand the succession of pastors, it should be noted that these priests were essentially working with a still growing, up-and-coming community that was intent on keeping German tradition. The diocese didn't offer much guidance to the priests on how to manage the situation they were being sent into. Furthermore, this rapid succession occurred during the American Civil War, which had an unprecedented impact on the country as a whole. Although the settlers of Grosse Pointe pre-date the Civil War, there were so few living in the area that it seems very few, if any, fought in the war.*(4)

To understand the swift turnover, it's best to address each of these men individually:

- **Father J.B.U. Jacoment** was appointed in 1852, but abruptly left after a mere two months. It is assumed he was not welcomed by the Germans. Upon his exit, St. Joseph's lost its "parish" title and was reverted back to a "mission." Perhaps this was done as punishment by the Chicago Diocese, although history does not confirm. We can assume this removal of the "parish" title only angered the St. Joseph parishioners more.

- **Father Lawrence Kuepfer** was appointed in the Fall of 1852 with the "parish" title reinstated, yet he exited six months later.

- **Father Nicholas Stauder** was appointed in 1853, but left in 1855. As with the two previous short-term pastors, there are no details concerning his tenure. It is assumed that Fr. Stauder was also not welcomed by the parishioners of St. Joseph's and/or didn't like the wilderness of Grosse Pointe.

---

* The only Civil War anecdote about Grosse Pointe was that the railroad men had made note of the numbers of dead being brought up from the south to their home farms in Wisconsin.

- **Father Anthony Kopp**, vicar general to the Chicago Diocese, was appointed pastor in 1855. Fr. Kopp was reported to be generous with his time to the fragile and rugged area; his tenure is marked with tranquility, discipline and continued growth. Fr. Kopp remained until August 19, 1860, as matters of the Chicago Diocese began to consume too much of his time.

- **Father Peter Kartlaub** was appointed pastor in 1860 but left before the end of the year.

- **Father Tschider** was appointed in January 1861, but left in June. He may have simply been an "administrator," as his name only appears in only one St. Joseph anthology's pastor listing.

- **Father Franz Blaesinger** was appointed pastor sometime in 1861 and remained for three years until November 1864. No details about St. Joseph's Parish are evident at this time. Given that Fr. Blaesinger's tenure was during the intense years of the American Civil War, the attention of the country was likely fixated elsewhere.

- **Redemptorist Priests**, a religious order based out of St. Michael's Parish from the city of Chicago, was assigned responsibility of St. Joseph's (but probably had already been assisting at the parish before Fr. Blaesinger left). Three priests (Father Majerus, Father Hahn and Father Schaefler) rotated religious duties to St. Joseph's for a year until the early 1865.

The Unfortunate Case of Fr. Bernard Heskemann

By all accounts, Fr. Blaesinger's three-year tenure was peaceful, yet his unexplained departure in November 1864 disrupted St. Joseph's again, and this time it truly infuriated the parishioners.

It's important to realize that a community of foreigners will display more resistance to change and government bureaucracy, particularly when the group of foreigners has been toiling away on creating their own localized government and farming economy. It's even more difficult when the *religious hierarchy* are the ones initiating and perpetuating the bureaucracy.

There is a trend displayed throughout St. Joseph's succession of pastors; they either remain for a very short period of time, or they stay for a handful of years and leave while the parish erupts into disarray. This reflects levels of discontent on both St. Joseph's and the Diocese of Chicago; removing the spiritual leader dislodges the community and the job therefore becomes harder to fill.

Due to the exit of Fr. Blaesinger, St. Joseph's had to rely on priests from an entirely different parish;

St. Michael's was 16 miles south and was staffed by Redemptorists (priests of the Congregation of the Most Holy Redeemer religious order).

In June of 1865, responding to an urgent request for Anointing of the Sick, Father Bernard Heskemann arrived to Grosse Pointe and was instantly impressed with the beauty of the area. It was obvious to Fr. Heskemann that St. Joseph's was in dire need of a full-time spiritual leader, and so he volunteered his service to the parish on a more permanent basis. This willingness to address the problems at hand made Fr. Heskemann an instant leading contender to shepherd the Catholics of St. Joseph's and the Grosse Pointe area.

On October 18, 1865, Fr. Heskemann was appointed pastor, beginning what many anticipated to be a promising future - yet Fr. Heskemann's tenure would end with an embarrassing tragedy that risked the entire dissolvement of St. Joseph's parish.

***

There are more notes in the parish archives during Fr. Heskemann's tenure than any of the previous pastors before him. This indicates that under Fr. Heskemann's leadership, St. Joseph's became a more vibrant parish filled with activity - something that the other pastors are not credited with. Similar to Fr. Fortmann's tenure, there was an increase in religious ceremonies and devout practices which caused other faithful Catholics to flock to Grosse Pointe and participate in the services. The property of St. Joseph's itself was growing, as a new log cabin rectory sprang up sometime in 1866.

A little over two years into Fr. Heskemann's leadership, on January 26, 1868, it was decided that St. Joseph's would build a new formal church to replace the log cabin. The estimated cost came to $20,000, but the parishioners only *pledged* $12,000 throughout 1868. Over the next four years, there were three economic reasons that factored into leaving St. Joseph's Parish with very bleak prospects:

First - beginning construction on a brand new pristine church with an estimated $8,000 short of pledges was a very risky financial decision, if not totally reckless, considering that the initial $12,000 was *pledged* money and not hard cash. By modern economic inflation, that $8,000 could be seen as anywhere from $130,000 to $200,000. Since the Grosse Pointe area was growing, the parishioners had assumed that the missing funds would eventually be acquired. Nevertheless, it was poor judgement on the part of St. Joseph's Parish to begin a substantial construction project lacking approximately 40% of the budget needed for completion.

Second - there were a number of events that resulted in money tightening throughout the late 1860s and early 1870s. The United States was in the

Reconstruction Era, particularly the "radical reconstruction" phase. Two years after the end of the Civil War, the federal government had decided to become more involved with changing laws in the southern states, drastically affecting the south's economic structure. Additionally, the Reconstruction Era resulted in more taxes which further bound people's wallets. On a global level, the Panic of 1866 which began in London was gradually being felt in America as well (although much more significantly a couple of years later). Finally, on a local level, the Franco-Prussian War, while having no effect on local monetary matters, did absorb the attention of the German Grosse Pointe villagers.

Third - these economic hardships meant that the pledges were losing their monetary value. Two events happened next (although records don't indicate which happened first); with the church already in construction and funds falling short, it risked not being completed. The frantic parochial committee resorted to taking out loans to finish the building - and these loans came with extremely high interest rates. At some point in late 1871, they eventually decided to halt construction due to the skyrocketing cost of the building. This unexpected halt in production meant that a rudimentary flat roof was substituted on the building, which created an odd sight on the horizon of Ridge Road. Due to the high interest loans, this half-finished, unfurnished and bizarre looking church plummeted St. Joseph's Parish in a $15,000 debt (with present-day inflation, this would be over $280,000).

Another indicator that trouble was on the horizon was that 65 families broke away from St. Joseph's, changing one of their earlier "mission sites" into it's own parish. In May of 1869, St. Peter's Catholic Parish was established just over four miles south of St. Joseph's in present-day Skokie. Although there were many Germans in the entire Grosse Pointe area, the fact that a new Catholic parish was founded along one of the main trails does indicate that people were outgrowing St. Joseph's.(5)

Ultimately, St. Joseph Parish's naiveté had really been to blame, but Fr. Heskemann took personal responsibility for the mess. He blamed himself and started to appear "extremely neurotic [and] frightfully despondent."(6) Fr. Heskemann was consumed by despair and boxed himself into a state of constant guilt. By modern understanding, it is believed that Fr. Heskemann had a mental breakdown. He abandoned his pastorship and declared that he wanted to live out the rest of his life in solace.

Although this picture was probably taken in the 1890s or early 1900s, the steeple of St. Joseph's is visible on right hand side of the street – an example of how prominent the church looked from afar in the neighborhood.

Part II

Preface to
Part II

The life of a president is well documented. Their entire biography is examined prior to being elected, and each day their decisions on any given topic is recorded for history and analyzed by political pundits. The life of a music celebrity or a movie star is loaded with interviews, collaborative witnesses and actual "art" to examine them from. The life of a canonized saint is meticulously studied by religious leaders, and the life of an infamous criminal is deeply researched by police.

Father William Netstraeter offers no writings. There are no recorded sermons. There are no interviews. There is no one alive who remembers him. The quotes that do exist are likely paraphrases. His last will and testament was likely written with the assistance of a lawyer.

Consider also his line of work: a parish priest and real estate developer. Particularly in a semi-rural territory as Grosse Pointe, these careers were not well documented. Although Fr. Netstraeter was responsible for the growth of the north shore and his land sales are (somewhat) recorded, that area of Chicago will not be studied with the same fascination or attention as downtown Chicago. Although he dabbled in politics, small local government meetings are not recorded with the same level of detail as that of Washington D.C. politics.

Finally, the time frame of Fr. Netstraeter's pastorate spans from the 1870s to the 1920s, a time where little documentation about neighborhood parish life exists as is. For 52 of his 83 years, Fr. Netstraeter remained in one specific location, isolating his actions in and around St. Joseph's Parish. In other words, the parish and local history experts have been able to incubate his biography and all its details. In fact, it's probably because Fr. Netstraeter remained in one place for so long that his full life's work *can* be examined.

***

These circumstances require that Fr. Netstraeter's biography be told a different way. Although it seems erroneous to not tell the story chronologically, the lack of details over a fifty-year time span causes subjects to constantly switch. Oftentimes a historical event occurs decades before it becomes relevant again, and in a long pastoral tenure that already lacks details, the jumping back and forth between topics is difficult to keep straight.

Therefore, Fr. Netstrater's biography will be presented in topics. We will look at his fifty-year-long legacy from the perspective of his priestly vows, his real estate development, and his political aspirations one at a time instead of trying to spool a yarn with a lack of details. It's much easier to "reset the clock" than to merge Fr. Netstraeter's biography into a sequential (and sporadic) presentation where significant events overlap.

Unlike the lives of Ulysses S. Grant, William McKinley or Teddy Roosevelt, which have been recorded in great detail as they were the most famous presidents during Fr. Netstraeter's lifetime - our lone priest's actions were not documented with the same level of attention. The early days of Evanston, Gross Point, Skokie, Wilmette and Winnetka did not have a robust news media that would report on local events.

In his lifetime, most of Fr. Netstraeter's actions were not deemed significant to record. Only in hindsight would their relevance become important.

Chapter Four
A Bargain

At the time when the first German Catholics were leaving their homes to cross the ocean for the new world and settle along Chicago's north shore forest, the man who would become the area's primary architect 30 years later was born.

The character of Fr. Netstraeter doesn't show up in St. Joseph's history books until the summer of 1872 when he was assigned to the distraught parish. Few (if any) books on the Village of Wilmette even acknowledge Fr. Netstraeter's existence. The mystery of who Fr. Netstraeter *was* prior to his pastorship of St. Joseph's contributes to the quasi-mythical lore of his appearance: a lone priest in a black cassock riding on horseback, trotting into the isolated village, a stranger intent on greeting every single person in Wilmette as his first inaugural act of being their shepherd.

Prior to his arrival, Fr. Netstraeter's biography is largely unknown. Essentially the first three decades of his life are almost a complete blank. There is no extended family lineage, no details about his youth, or list of classes he took throughout his education. His first assignments as a priest seem to be lost in history. This lack of details in his early years would eventually become opportunity for an illegitimate claim on his life's work.

At the age of 31, Fr. Netstraeter's biography begins; peculiarly similar to how Jesus Christ's public life began when he was 30.

The First Thirty Years – What Little We Know (1841 to 1872)

On January 1, 1841, William Netstraeter was born to Franz Netstraeter and Maria Schulte in the town of Meschede, in the Westphalia region of Germany. When William was eight years old, his mother Maria died; his father Franz never remarried.

In 1863, at the age of 22, William entered the University of Münster. Two years later, in 1865, he attended the University of Paderborn to complete his college studies.

In late 1866 or possibly early 1867, he exited the University of Paderborn as a sub-deacon, and made his way over to the United States. William was admitted to St. Francis de Sales Seminary just south of Milwaukee on March 23, 1867. Four months later he was ordained a deacon on July 16, and then ordained a priest on September 30, 1867 in the Mater Christi Chapel of the Seminary. There is reason to believe that during the two and a half months between his ordination as a deacon and his ordination as a priest, William Netstraeter spent time in the Chicago Diocese, either at a parish or simply familiarizing himself with the diocese he would soon work for.[1]

Fr. Netstraeter's first assignment(s) are unknown; or rather, the details are sloppy and don't add up. Oddly, his name first appears in St. Joseph's Parish record book on Friday, October 11, 1867 - *less than two weeks after* his ordination. It appears again twice, on Sunday October 13, and again on Tuesday, October 15, 1867. Unless it was some sort of sacramental correction made years afterwards (which is *very unlikely* given that there are no notations regarding corrections), perhaps Fr. Netstraeter was assisting for a few days at St. Joseph's? This record suggests that he spent a short amount of time at St. Joseph's prior to his formal "black cassock on horseback" arrival as pastor. Wilmette historian George Bushnell believes that Fr. Netstraeter's first celebrations of the Mass were at St. Joseph's, and these notations give credence to Bushnell's claim. Additionally, Fr. Heskemann's name appears multiple times before and after these three entries. Perhaps the two met? Perhaps the two kept in contact? Was Fr. Netstraeter aware of the financial drama unfolding?

We know that Fr. Netstraeter was sent approximately 150 miles south to the city of Bloomington, where there were also pockets of German

Catholics living throughout the area. Historian Mark Dunn's research indicates that:

> On Sunday, October 4, 1868, Father Netstraeter was in Bloomington, assisted with the Confirmations and participated in the dedication ceremony. Over 4,000 people reportedly attended these ceremonies.(2)

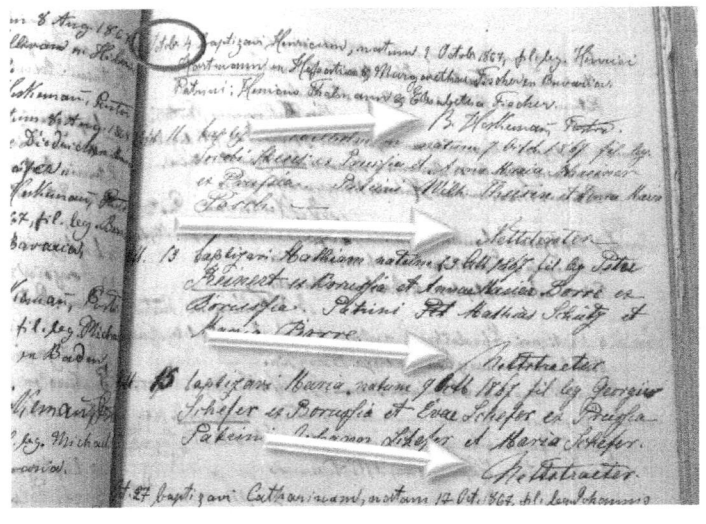

A page from the actual register. When looking up 1867, we see a notation signed with "B. Heskemann" on October 4. The next three entries are all "Netstraeter." Fr. Netstraeter's name does not appear in this book again until the summer of 1872.

We know that at some point, in either 1868 or 1869, Fr. Netstraeter was sent an additional 30 miles south to Lincoln, Illinois,* where it was reported he was pastor of St. Mary's Catholic Church, although his installation date as pastor of St. Mary's is unknown. Due to the merging of Catholic parishes in the 2000s and 2010s, the history has gotten incredibly tangled and harder to track down.

The Diocese Makes An Offer
(May 1872)

Due to the crisis erupting at St. Joseph's, Bishop Thomas Foley of the Chicago Diocese reached out to the young German priest. Bishop Foley offered a bargain to Fr. Netstraeter: relocate 180 miles north to St. Joseph's as pastor and reign in the frantic parish to some degree of stability. Being that Fr. Netstraeter is from the same region (Trier) as the founding parishioners, the appointment made sense. If Fr. Netstraeter agreed and remained at St. Joseph's for two years, he would be rewarded with a pastorship in the city of Chicago.

To be pastor of a church in the city of Chicago was very desirable, at least when compared with the

---

* The town of "Lincoln" was named after Abraham Lincoln on August 27, 1853, when he first purchased plots on what was to be a new town. This was seven years before Lincoln was elected president. No one knows exactly how the name "Lincoln" was chose, although historians believe that Abraham Lincoln would *not* have named the town after himself.

Bishop Thomas P. Foley

backwoods area of St. Joseph's. Although the Grosse Point area was rapidly becoming more cultured, a parish so far removed from the hub of "action" (i.e. Chicago) was probably not appealing to most young men. Also, the amount of debt that the parish collected, particularly in America's Reconstruction Era, was a mess few priests would want to deal with. Finally, there is little doubt that St. Joseph's reputation for scaring away pastors was a secret; few priests want to "shepherd" a parish where they don't have control, or rather, where the "sheep" make the calls. Additionally, Bishop Foley only asked/appointed Fr. Netstraeter for two years. Hence, it was another short-term appointment that would have likely upset the parishioners *again* once the pastor moved on.

Considering the outstanding success Fr. Netstraeter had, one might wonder if he saw an opportunity? Since history only gives us an account of his *actions* to study, we can ponder a variety of questions: Did Fr. Netstraeter accept the job because he wanted a larger Chicago parish, and then changed his mind after arriving to St. Joseph's? Did Fr. Netstraeter see a golden opportunity to create his own pseudo-empire? Did he fear the aggressive parishioners? Or, did he dismiss the idea of a challenge because he was one of them? Did he prefer the quiet and separated atmosphere of Grosse Pointe from the loud city? Did the parishioners persuade Fr. Netstraeter to stay when his two years were up?

There are lengthy answers to these questions, and the studies of religious pastorship, American economic history and Chicago history would have to be considered in trying to come up with an answer. The fact remains that Fr. Netstraeter accepted the assignment, but never got the other side of the offer. He stayed at St. Joseph's and remained there for 52 years.

St. Joseph the Worker & Fr. William Netstraeter

There are some peculiar biographical details about St. Joseph the Worker that parallel Fr. Netstraeter's life. Joseph's first historical appearance is in the remote village of Nazareth. This is true with the bulk of Fr. Netstraeter's historical biography, which is scarce until arriving in remote Wilmette. Catholic tradition believes that Joseph migrated from one location to another during "The Flight to Egypt", just like Fr. Netstraeter's constant movements from Germany to Wisconsin, from southern Illinois to Chicago.

Yet the most provocative parallel to Joseph the Worker is through the profession of carpentry. Woodwork requires a significant amount of time, dedication, and careful hands-on labor. Upon Fr. Netstraeter's assignment to Grosse Pointe, he went *directly* to the core of the parish through visiting each individual home in the neighborhood on horseback. He sought to establish himself as *their* pastor, giving those he visited words of solace and encouragement. Fr. Netstraeter was showing the parishioners that he would take a hands-on approach to mending St. Joseph's Parish.

Incorporation

Later in the same summer that Fr. Netstraeter arrived, the locals decided that it was time to create a new village. The municipal needs of the area required governmental organization, and so on August 15, 1872, a meeting was held at the train station. The incorporation referendum vote won, with 37 for and 7 against the creation of the Village of Wilmette.* The name of *Wilmette* came from the French Ouilmette family who were the first white Europeans to purchase land on the lake shore in the 1790s. At this time, The

---

* Technically, September 19, 1872 was the formal "birthdate" when 26 people were elected to the board of trustees.

Village of Wilmette had only 300 residents living in its territory.

The fact that Wilmette formally established itself the same summer that the "godfather" of the village arrived was a prophetic foreshadowing of events to come.

Chapter Five
Renovation:
St. Joseph's Parish Under Fr. Netstraeter's Leadership

When ordained a priest, William Netstraeter took a vow to devote himself to the work of Christ: spreading the Gospel, teaching the faith, administering the sacraments, evangelizing and bringing everyone closer into the Church. His appointment as pastor of St. Joseph's in Wilmette was his primary concern, and although he actively participated in politics and real estate, those endeavors ultimately funneled back into St. Joseph's. He was a priest first. His main priority was to be St. Joseph's shepherd, yet he acted as a "shepherd" to all, regardless of territory or religious beliefs. His tenure as mayor, the buying and selling of land, and his involvement with other local parishes all supported the creation and growth of a sanguine community.

The Great Chicago Fire & Aftermath

As St. Joseph's Parish was spiraling into financial instability, the greater Chicagoland area was consumed by a drastic event.

On the evening of October 8, 1871, a fire broke out in the city's present-day "south loop" area. Within the course of 24 hours, the fire devoured an incredible stretch of the city, measuring at 4 miles long (north & south) and 0.75 miles wide (east & west). Over 17,500 buildings were destroyed; only 7 remained standing after the blaze was put out. The fire resulted in the destruction of two prominent downtown churches[1] in which many of the early Diocesan records were lost; hence, a possible reason why some details about St. Joseph's earlier years are missing.

Despite the incredible spread of destruction, many people had time to escape from the fire's path, which is why the death toll was approximately 300[2], significantly lower than anticipated for a disaster of that magnitude. However, the Great Chicago Fire resulted in leaving at least 95,000 people homeless, which was well over 25% of the city's residents, possibly closer to 30%[3]. Many camped out in what is today the Lincoln Park neighborhood, and because the waterworks were destroyed, some had to resort to Lake Michigan and old wells. Chicago fell victim to looters and vandals, resulting in Mayor Roswell Mason placing the city under martial law (which only lasted a few weeks).

Immediately following the fire, many traveled from neighboring areas to assist with the rebuilding, and donations quickly began pouring in. The majority of displaced people were determined to rebuild; even some

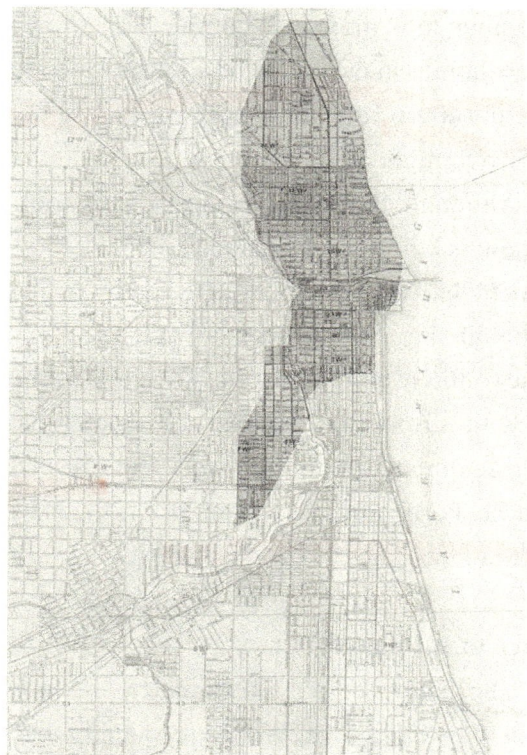

The shaded part of the map indicates the fire's path of destruction.

temporary shops were set up within days after the fire. As Chicago's eastern border is a water mass (Lake Michigan), homeless could only relocate south, west or northbound. Due to this sudden dispersing of people, literally overnight, as well as the influx of construction and national attention the city received, the momentum of the Chicago economy drastically increased. The city's cleanup took months to complete, so some people made new homes in the extended Chicagoland area. The "American suburb" did not simply appear – it became a necessity overnight.

Although the Great Chicago Fire took place seven months before Fr. Netstraeter arrived, the Village of Wilmette had certainly been affected by this tragedy. Even though Fr. Netstraeter was specifically sent to serve the Catholic population, the village as a whole was rocked with turmoil and struck with a combination of anger, resentment, frustration and fear. As with the beloved Fr. Fortmann thirty years prior, Fr. Netstraeter focused on nurturing the people's spirit.

Evidence of Influence

The sight of Fr. Netstraeter on horseback traveling the Village of Wilmette quickly became a familiar sight. The most colorful retelling, and probably the origin of the "priest on horseback" narrative, comes from Rev. F. L. Kalvelage's extensive history of St. Joseph's parish:

> From great distances, even the children were able to recognize the lone horseman, and they would pause in their play to gleefully announce to the family that the priest was on the way. Mother and father joined the children in joyous anticipation. Upon his arrival the entire family enjoyed

> a recess from their respective tasks and sat
> around Father Netstraeter listening intently
> to the words of solace and encouragement.
> He was *their pastor*; they were *his* flock.(4)

The passage is arguably fictitious in tone, yet considering the impact of the Great Chicago Fire, the rampant debt of St. Joseph's and the mental strain of those living in the Grosse Pointe region, the village was in need of healing. The level of stress affecting those in St. Joseph's demanded emotional support just as much as financial.

Fr. Netstraeter's attention went to the completion of the unfinished building project that his predecessor began. None of the records indicate exactly how or when the dilapidated roof of the new church was finished(5), although each historical record suggests that the church was completed within the same year Fr. Netstraeter arrived. This accomplishment is financially unexplainable and the parish history books quickly move past it, citing it as an indicator of Fr. Netstraeter's instantly good relationship with the parishioners.

One of the most popular stories that displays Fr. Netstraeter's influence comes less than six months after his assignment to the parish. In his decision to put aside the parish bureaucracy in lieu of the "people," he made an effort to be a spiritual counselor to the "flock." An example of this gratitude was seen on October 1, 1872, when Anton Poesch graciously cancelled his debt of $1,394 to St. Joseph's Parish (an amount that would certainly exceed $25,000 by modern inflation rates). There has never been a formal explanation as to why Mr. Poesch performed such a gracious act, but he and Fr. Netstraeter remained friends throughout the years and would continue to do business together.

Anton Poesch would become one Fr. Netstraeter's regular collaborators and arguably one of the greatest contributors in the history of St. Joseph's.

The Panic of 1873

On September 8, 1873, just over a year into Fr. Netstraeter's pastorate, the United States' economy began slipping into a depression that triggered concerns throughout the country. By September 20, the fear had gotten so bad that the New York stock exchange paused trading for ten days. As articulated by historian Ron Chernow:

> The crisis was deep and intractable and persisted for more than five brutal years. It would be termed "the Great Depression" until eclipsed by the 1930s downturn. Much of the industrial landscape lay in ruins: half the nation's railroads went into receivership and half of its iron furnaces shut down. In farming areas, crop and land prices plunged. In New York City alone, a quarter of all workers were tossed from their jobs. Before the depression ran its course, deflation had dragged down wholesale prices by 30 percent. Industrial leaders banded together to cut production and stabilize prices, leading to monopolistic practices in many industries and spawning a corresponding concentration in labor. Many workers joined unions that engaged in railway, textile, and coal strikes and flirted with radical movements.(6)

Prior to this crisis, the American economy appeared healthy with an increase in industry, particularly through the railways. However, this economic surplus proved to be the result of overly positive thinking by those viewing the economy through rose-colored spectacles. Essentially, the generous amounts of credit had overextended the nation's railroads.

Therefore, it's really no surprise that when America's economy *appeared* to be getting stronger five years prior, the St. Joseph parishioners would embark on the ambitious task of building a new formal church. Given St. Joseph's Parish's own financial downturn in 1871 and 1872, compounded with this unforeseen depression the following year, the church seemed destined to either close down or require a hefty bailout from the Chicago Diocese. Considering the sad state of affairs that Fr. Netstraeter walked into, it's bizarrely remarkable that during his first few years, there was growth at St. Joseph's! The parish did not simply get by; it revolutionized.

The Teacher

Also in 1873, the second year of Fr. Netstraeter's pastorate, a entirely new frame school building was constructed and added to the back side of the church. It is believed that Fr. Netstraeter initiated this new construction project to comply with provisions from two Plenary Councils that highlighted the establishment of Catholic Schools within the parish community.(7) Three years later, in 1876, a second floor was added to the school building for housing teachers on-site. By the following September (1877), the School Sisters of St. Francis of Milwaukee had arrived to assume teaching responsibilities. These were nuns from the same seminary that Fr. Netstraeter attended for his final months before ordination.(8) Fr. Netstraeter himself taught a daily class in the school; although no syllabus or schedule exists, we assume it was a religion class.

He even taught a one-hour Sunday afternoon religion class for students who completed their "primary education" (grades first through eighth). This Sunday afternoon class was part of a devotion Fr. Netstraeter asked of the children on completion of their First Communion: that for three consecutive years after their "primary education" was finished, they would continue these extracurricular religion classes. These Sunday afternoon lessons reflect the concept of placing emphasis on religious devotion. As with former pastors Fr. Fortmann and Fr. Heskemann, the increase of religious devotion allows the parish community to thrive.

Construction In and Around St. Joseph's

Within his first five years as pastor, Fr. Netstraeter fixed the dilapidated church roof and oversaw an entirely new school building added to the back of the church. He then enlarged it to house teachers. These three achievements alone were Herculean tasks that would have easily earned Fr.

Netstraeter the desired pastorship in the city of Chicago (should he want to "cash in" on Bishop Foley's offer). However, they were the first of a series of construction projects that Fr. Netstraeter would undertake throughout his pastorate:

1881 - Although the troublesome church finally got a roof, it was never properly furnished. Nine years later, the church received its first renovation and was properly decorated.

1886 - As with the first two log cabin churches, the exact placement of the first rectory on the St. Joseph property is not known. What we do know is that the rectory was moved closer to the school building in a vacant lot and converted into a convent for nuns. Fr. Netstraeter oversaw the building of a new rectory across the street (Lake Street) from the church/school.

1892 - A three-story building was erected at the rear of the church, with four classrooms and an auditorium. It is not clear if this building was *added* or *a replacement* onto the frame structure from the mid-1870s.

1915 - Twenty-three years passed between Fr. Netstraeter's extensive construction projects and the last during his lifetime. A new school made with fireproof materials went up with many classrooms and an auditorium. Anton Poesch covered 80% of the cost for this massive project.

***

Sadly, none of these buildings are in existence today. The old church, the old school, the old convent and the old rectory were all torn down by 1939. The Mallinckrodt Center (more in the next chapter) was finished in 1914 and is the only remaining building from the era that Fr. Netstraeter had some involvement with. For reference, the current church of St. Peter's in Skokie (the parish started by the extended German farmers from St. Joseph's) was built in 1894 and still stands. St. Peter's in Skokie is probably the most similar in shape, size and scope (positioned in a prominent downtown area) to the original St. Joseph's church in Wilmette.

Fr. Netstraeter's final edifice would not arrive until *fifteen years* after his death.

The nuns inside the window frames as the new school was under construction

St. Joseph School, Class of 1890.

St. Joseph's School

A classroom inside St. Joseph's School

Some of these pamphlets from the early 1900s still exist.

St. Joseph's in Wilmette (left), circa late 1870s and St. Peter's in Skokie (right) in 2019. St. Joseph's church was completed in 1873, but was torn down in 1938. The current St. Peter's church, 4 miles southwest, was built in 1894 and still stands. St. Peter's is the most similar to the original St. Joseph's.

The interior of St. Joseph's church after the late 1880s refurbishing.

St. Joseph Cemetery, taken (circa) 1897 to document a special occasion – presumed Memorial Day due to the large crowd, some of whom are dressed in mourning clothes with some holding U.S. flags. Many of the area's earliest settlers are buried in this cemetery. The Wilmette Historical Museum believes that this print reverses the original; the building entrance visible at the right is actually the church, which was south of the cemetery.

The New World

There is a small anecdote in Fr. Netstraeter's biography that appears in two of St. Joseph's history books (the 1939 and 2010 editions) that's worth highlighting, as it pays credit to his financial wisdom. Bishop Patrick Feehan started the Archdiocesan newspaper, *The New World*, in 1892 and appointed Fr. Netstraeter to the board of the newspaper as treasurer. Despite all the work Fr. Netstraeter undertook in local government, he never dabbled in journalism or the press. Furthermore, since English was Fr. Netstraeter's second language, he would not have been appointed for his linguistic or journalistic abilities, but rather for his financial expertise. There is belief that *The New World* was in financial trouble at the time of his appointment and Fr. Netstraeter's reputation as a financial master was noticed by Bishop Feehan - but this is unconfirmed.(9)

Franz Netstraeter

There are few details about Fr. Netstraeter's father, Franz. We know that he never remarried after Maria died in 1851 and that he arrived to the United States in 1867(10), the same year that William arrived, which suggests that they traveled together. We can reasonably assume that Franz associated with the older members of St. Joseph's community.

The earliest photograph of Fr. Netstraeter is a "mourning portrait" of him and Franz. The mourning portrait was a way of making a memorial of a loved one - a practice unheard of in the modern era, yet common among European Americans in the 1800s and early 1900s (some cultures still do this). Additionally, as death was more common in the home and photography was a long and expensive process, it was likely the only photograph of some who lived in the 1800s. Franz died on June 18, 1907 and was buried in St. Joseph's cemetery.

The earliest known photograph of Fr. Netstraeter (right) is an eerie "mourning portrait" with his deceased father, Franz (left).

Chapter Six
Boomtown:
Selling Wilmette to Chicago

This area of Fr. Netstraeter's biography is considered the most unusual by contemporary understanding of Catholic clergy. Even his political activism - addressed in the following chapter - is not altogether uncommon when considering the modern-day Catholic church. While there are no regulations against a Catholic priest engaging in a side business, the practice is uncommon, and in most cases these "side jobs" are hobbies or church related (such as a teaching position or a canon lawyer).

The concept of a parish rectory as a pseudo-real estate office needs to be examined in proper context: Fr. Netstraeter's business transactions were what was expected of a parish priest in Germany.

There is an additional theory of why he chose real estate as a business practice. It was no secret that the parishioners of St. Joseph's were a troublesome group. They had become disgruntled with the previous pastors, so it would be naive to not anticipate that the drama would play out again. Mark Dunn makes the poignant observation that:

> It seems apparent that Father Nestraeter's early approach at St. Joseph was intended to clearly establish his own authority, quell his own "strong-willed" parishioners, and gain control of the parish finances. What he did over the next fifty years in lending money and investing in real estate was far more than a hobby. He consciously intended to strengthen his hand in managing and controlling the parish finances as part of this broader obligations to the German Catholic parish he had been entrusted to lead.[1]

The real estate dealings are a financial explanation as to how the parish turned around. Not to underscore the emphasis placed on worship, religious education and Fr. Netstraeter's own personal relationship with the parishioners, these business transactions can be viewed as a physical representation of his success. Similar to what the early pioneers and settlers were doing in the mid-1800s — buying and selling land — Fr. Netstraeter continued the tradition in a modernized way. He began acquiring land within a mile radius of the parish grounds, both in Wilmette and Gross Point, and he would also offer mortgages.

Boomtown 107

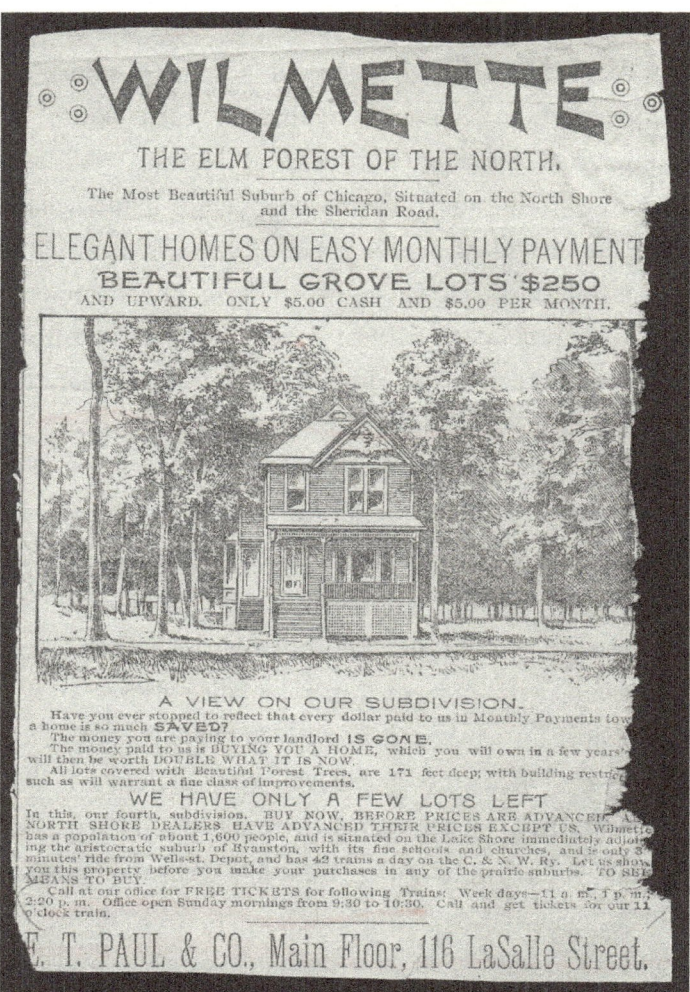

Although this is not one of Fr. Netstraeter's advertisements, this newspaper clipping is an example of ads placed in various Chicago newspapers trying to "sell" the Village of Wilmette to potential residents.

Any sort of detailed listing of Fr. Netstraeter's real estate transactions are blurred by time. To use the old deeds and titles in St. Joseph's archives and then reconcile them against a listing of each house in Wilmette, differentiate houses from the former Village of Gross Point, and find any changes in homeowners over the course of over a hundred years is a virtually impossible task. However, we believe Fr. Netstraeter began his practice in earnest in 1881, buying land from the parishioners of St. Joseph's. The same year, he purchased an acre of land from his friend Anton Poesch. There is no formal explanation as to where Fr. Netstraeter had the funds to launch his mortgage practice, but we can deduce that since he was a shrewd businessman throughout his entire life, he had finances secluded for real estate. Additionally, his father Franz had been with him in America since 1867 so it's reasonable to assume they arrived with a surplus of finances. Once the business was underway and successful, Fr. Netstraeter took the steps to "sell" the Village of Wilmette to Catholics in the greater Chicagoland area. Regular ads were placed in the Sunday Chicago Tribune inviting Catholics to move to the Wilmette area.

Mallinckrodt: The Water Treat Faux Pas
The Early 1890s - Mother Alexia, the Mother Superior of the nuns who taught at St. Joseph's school, had been

suffering from rheumatism. Sometime in the late 1880s or early 1890s, she traveled overseas to Bavaria, Germany for a special "cold water" treatment. At the time, water treatments for arthritis and stiffness were considered cutting-edge for elders; therefore the practice was growing in popularity.

Upon her return to Wilmette, Mother Alexia suggested the idea of building a water treatment facility in the area; no doubt it would become a source of revenue. Additionally, Mother Alexia was fully aware of what Fr. Netstraeter was accomplishing with real estate in the local area, and he supported the idea.[2]

The proposal was to build the water sanitarium in Gross Point, no more than a block or two north of St. Joseph's. On October 31, 1892, the Franciscans (i.e. School Sisters) purchased thirty acres for $20,000, with an adjoining seven acres from Father Netstraeter himself. In mid-December, Fr. Netstraeter appeared before Wilmette's Board asking permission to extend Wilmette's sewer system across Ridge Road into this new property in Gross Point. As historian Mark Dunn points out:

> As a two-time President of that board, he [Fr. Netstraeter] probably expected favorable treatment. Instead, all hell broke loose, and by the time the Board met on January 5, 1893, ninety-five citizens had

filed a petition in opposition to the proposed sewer connection.(3)

The intense rejection of Fr. Netstraeter and Mother Alexia's proposed sewer plans and water treatment facility had nothing to do with them personally. Rather, the backlash was fueled by a controversy from years previous, when Cook County was clandestinely attempting to place an insane asylum near the shore line of Lake Michigan. Obviously, an insane asylum is not a desired facility in a suburban neighborhood, much less in the 1890s, when security was nowhere near as advanced as it is today and the treatment of the mentally ill was rudimentary and generally ineffective. Cook County clearly wanted to install the "asylum" or "treatment center" in secret, but once the scheme was discovered, Wilmette strongly pushed back against it.

Hence, despite their influence and popularity, Fr. Netstraeter and Mother Alexia were roundly defeated due to a misunderstanding of words. News that Wilmette's new sewer system would be used for a water "asylum" or medical "facility" of any kind instantly ignited a negative reaction. It didn't matter that water "treatment" was used to curtail a physical ailment that primarily affected the elderly; the concept of any medical facility put villagers on edge. Without water, the sanitarium could not be built in Gross Point (the

Franciscans eventually built a water treatment facility in Milwaukee).

The Mid-1910s - For the next twenty years the majority of land was left empty. Fr. Netstraeter would use a portion of it for his own real estate practices, but the property closest to St. Joseph's remained untouched. As the taverns were quickly populating the "wet" side of Ridge Road (i.e. Gross Point's city boundaries), Fr. Netstraeter was not going to relinquish the land where more saloons would likely appear. Despite the assured monetary success of selling the land to potential business owners, it remained barren. The presence of the taverns, let alone so many of them, was viewed as a moral embarrassment to the traditionally Catholic area, and by the 1910s, Fr. Netstraeter was embroiled in a political fight against the sale of alcohol in Gross Point.

Certainly with the intention (in part) of trying to discourage the drunken behavior, Fr. Netstraeter encouraged the Sisters of Christian Charity from Pennsylvania to build on the vacant land where the proposed water treatment *was* supposed to go. In 1912, the Franciscan Sisters resold the land to the Sisters of Christian Charity. Within four years a new motherhouse and an all girls high school were constructed on the property and completed by 1916. The convent was called Maria Immaculata and the high school was called

Mallinckrodt, after the foundress of the Sisters, Pauline von Mallinckrodt.

The Early 2000s - Less than ten years after the completion of the Mallinckrodt building, the taverns had disappeared and the Village of Gross Point was no more.

The Mallinckrodt building would eventually be owned by Loyola University as a campus in Wilmette for a majority of the second half of the 1900s.

The property would see its final controversy in the new millennium when Loyola University planned to sell the campus to a developer who intended to demolish the building and replace it with single-family homes. In late 2001, a coalition of open land advocates, historic building preservationists and proponents of senior housing banded together, petitioning the Village of Wilmette to purchase the Mallinckrodt College property, including the 14 acre park behind the building. On March 19, 2002, a referendum was held, and Wilmette residents voted in favor of granting the local Park District authority to purchase the property. After a year and a half of monetary negotiations, the agreement was finalized in July 2004. The majority of the building would be converted into condominiums for senior citizens, and the facilities on the first floor would be incorporated into the Wilmette Park District for community use.

***

The entire land on which the Mallinckrodt building and the park rests, was intended to be a specialty center for seniors ended. It ended up serving multiple purposes until it finally became a *version* of what it was intended for. Portions of the land would be sold off to homeowners in the growing Village of Wilmette. The regal gothic-esque building was used for education, not sold for commercial business. In its lifetime, hundreds of students passed through the halls of Mallinckrodt at varying age levels. Although in the modern era, the Mallinckrodt Center doesn't offer late-1800s water therapy, it is a state-of-the-art retirement facility and serves Wilmette through the community Park District.

No doubt Fr. Netstraeter and Mother Alexia were disappointed when they were vehemently denied permission to use the area as originally intended, but circumstances outside of their control directed it towards other noteworthy purposes. The priest and the nun would not live to see the Village of Wilmette come to the defense of *"their"* building in 2001, but Mallinckrodt did successfully (and ironically) became a version of what Fr. Netstraeter & Mother Alexia intended it to be in their lifetime.

Mallinckrodt would not the only circumstance of when Fr. Netstraeter's intentions were in motion beyond the grave.

The Mallinckrodt building, circa 1920s. The land directly behind the building (west) is a 14-acre park that still exists today. Behind the park, another quarter mile west, was land that was used for real estate, the majority of which was under Fr. Netstraeter's supervision. In the bottom left hand corner of the photo, St. Joseph's cemetery can be seen.

Our Lady of Perpetual Help in Glenview

In the first decade of the 1900s, there were some Catholic families living west of Wilmette and Gross Point in the Village of Glenview. At the time, St. Joseph's was the closest church for them to attend Sunday Mass, which was a journey of anywhere from 4 to 6 miles, depending on the location of their farm. Considering that these farmers traveled either on foot or horse & carriage, the travel time to St. Joseph's was well over an hour. Concurrently, priests would need to travel to the Glenview area to minister the sacraments if needed.

In circa 1907, eighteen Glenview families petitioned Fr. Netstraeter to build a new church in their neighborhood, to which he agreed. Fr. Netstraeter purchased a plot of land on Grove Street, in what is today downtown Glenview, and oversaw the construction of a small church that could seat about 90 people. At the time, this became another "St. Joseph's Mission", located about four and half miles away from St. Joseph's in Wilmette. On November 1, 1907, "St Joseph's Mission" was dedicated. In 1915, the mission was renamed Our Lady of Perpetual Help (OLPH), and officially upgraded to a "parish" in 1919.

The old OLPH church, one of Fr. Netstraeter's construction projects outside of the Wilmette area. The building was torn down in 1949.

Memorial Park Cemetery in Skokie

It's important to highlight that Catholics were not the only Christians settling into the neighboring villages. Back in the late 1860s, before St. Peter's in Skokie was established, a Lutheran church was established a mere three blocks away. By the 1900s, at least a dozen various Protestant churches were established in the surrounding villages of Evanston, Glenview, Gross Point, Skokie and Wilmette. By 1913, Fr. Netstraeter's business associate and friend Anton Poesch had died, but Fr. Netstraeter still had land that had originally been devised to him from Mr. Poesch about 1 mile south of St. Joseph's. As the majority of the lots in St. Joseph's cemetery were filling up, Fr. Netstraeter saw to it that this land would be set aside for non-Catholics. The idea was to have a cemetery for all, even regardless of faith, in anticipation of future generations. (4)

Years after Fr. Netstraeter's death, Memorial Park cemetery would become the primary Jewish cemetery on Chicago's north side.

Netstraeter's North Shore

Each of these real estate actions were done in Fr. Netstraeter's own name, which allowed him a significant amount of control over the business. He could be as scrupulous with clients as he wanted to and was evidently very successful; he never foreclosed on anyone. What remains most remarkable about this, particularly by modern standards, was that Fr. Netstraeter, the pastor of St. Joseph's Parish, never took a salary. Yes, the parish provided him a home, food and presumably a staff of some kind – yet he himself, the pastor, never received payment through his primary job.

Fr. Netstraeter's local business was done with the intention of drawing new people to Wilmette and new parishioners to St. Joseph's. From a clerical and ecumenical standpoint this makes sense: Fr. Netstraeter could saturate the neighborhood with residents with whom he would develop a personal relationship. He knew the types of people funneling into his parish/neighborhood who would help it grow. Any priest would love the opportunity to have that type of hands-on approach in essentially "creating" their congregation.

The main entrance to Memorial Park Cemetery in Skokie.

Chapter Seven
The Politician

When one examines the political life of Fr. Netstraeter, it's a reflection of the issues that would hallmark the American Midwest in the late 1800s and early 1900s. Considering how politically charged his posthumous life would become, it seems oddly appropriate that Fr. Netstraeter was politically active in his lifetime.

Proper Perspective

The phrase "Separation of Church and State" is often attributed to Thomas Jefferson; it endorses the idea that government and church hierarchy should function as two independent operations. Although the two establishments may work and/or agree in tandem on a given topic, the purpose of the "separation of church and state" was to protect one institution from having influence over the other.

Over the course of American history, this concept has developed into a reason to absolve religious institutions from taxes. For Catholic parishes to remain tax-free, a majority of them have restricted themselves from direct political endorsements.

Although political activism is somewhat common in the modern-day American Catholic Church*, the idea that any priest, minister, cleric, rabbi or imam could be elected to a government office is *totally* unheard of.

It is crucial to highlight that in the 1880s, Fr. Netstraeter was fulfilling a role that was *expected* of Catholic priests from the European tradition he grew up in. Fr. Netstraeter viewed the local government system as a way to further his priestly responsibility as a way of shepherding the parishioners (people) of Wilmette as well as neighboring Evanston and Skokie.

Additionally, Fr. Netstraeter arrives in Wilmette only seven years from the conclusion of the Civil War – during a period called the "reconstruction" era of American history (not to mention the aftermath of the Great Chicago Fire). Fr. Netstraeter's political efforts were truly in the spirit of Abraham Lincoln's famous words from the Gettysburg address: "…that this nation

---

* Political activism in the United States on the part of the contemporary Catholic Church is a regular occurrence, particularly through the USCCB (the United States Conference of Catholic Bishops). Additionally, individual Catholic priests and leaders have taken a public stance on the national scene for advocating on behalf of political issues. Famously, Father Michael Pfleger has regularly pushed for gun control and publicly supported Barack Obama. Father Frank Pavone has devoted his ministry to pushing pro-life legislation and publicly supported Donald J. Trump.

under God, shall have a new birth of freedom – and that government *of the people, by the people, for the people*…" The political activity that Fr. Netstraeter, a Catholic priest, undertook was purely "for the people." There are no accounts that confirm, let alone suggest, that Fr. Netstraeter had campaigned on behalf of Democrats or Republicans. Without a doubt, the man certainly would have been opinionated on such matters, but all history offers is the work done on Chicago's north shore area.

Trustee & Mayor

Reflection of Fr. Netstraeter's popularity in his first few years as pastor can be gauged by his election to the Wilmette Village Board. Given the atmosphere of Wilmette in its first decade and the prominence that St. Joseph's Parish and School had for the neighborhood (keeping in mind it was functioning for thirty years prior to the Wilmette government), a popular pastor would have a significant amount of influence.

Beginning in 1882, Fr. Netstraeter was elected as a Trustee to the Wilmette Village Board. The residents most likely voted him as a leader who could influence the managing of their municipal functions. He remained a trustee until the year 1886, when that year, he was voted to be head of the Wilmette Village Board, making him the mayor of Wilmette for a one-year term. There is some speculation that Fr. Netstraeter sought mayorship to help influence the Village of Gross Point to ban alcohol, although that wouldn't become a major issue until the turn of the century. Four years later in 1890, due to the death of the incumbent mayor, Fr. Netstraeter was again elected to head the Wilmette Village Board (i.e. mayor) for a second one-year term.

Image presumably taken in St. Joseph's rectory due to the chair. There are still at least a dozen chairs of the exact same style present in the rectory and in church storage.

The Annexation Club

By the 1890s, Wilmette's population had grown to 1,500 and was experiencing a sort of "growing pain" in this era. Wilmette was not sharing in the economic stimulus that their neighbor, Gross Point, was experiencing (detailed in the following chapter), nor was it as developed as their other neighbor, Evanston. George D. Bushnell sketches out this time period of Wilmette as such:

> The decade of the 1880s and 1890s saw Wilmette transformed from a scattered settlement of houses, surrounded by thick woods and huddled within a few blocks of the depot, to a rapidly growing Chicago suburb. During these 20 years, the village residents would establish basic organizations from social clubs to schools, to meet the needs of the community.(1)

During 1893 and 1894, there was a political push which seems unthinkable by modern measures since Fr. Netstraeter is recognized as a "founding father" of Wilmette – yet it displays the dynamics of the era.

Fr. Netstraeter was a leading member of a group called "The Annexation Club" that wanted to see the Village of Wilmette annexed to the larger Evanston. The move would have major benefits for the residents of

Wilmette, including access to the public high school, a share in the ownership of Evanston's water plant, lower taxes, electric street lights, as well as superior fire and police protection.(2)

Fr. Netstraeter was opposed by another group known as the "Wilmette Citizens Association," who argued that Wilmette was financially stable, should remain independent and thrive on its own integrity. Although it might seem odd to not join with an economically stronger village, the determination for some villagers to remain independent reflects a pride within the people of Wilmette.

The debate was put to a public forum on January 23, 1894, where the two groups debated their positions. Three months later, on April 10, a special election was held in Wilmette that defeated "The Annexation Club" 168 to 165; a mere three votes determined that Wilmette would remain independent. A week later, the larger Evanston held their own election on the subject and the results were 735 for consuming Wilmette, with 596 for Evanston remaining as is (roughly 3 against 2). Clearly the popular opinion of the area was to combine Wilmette and Evanston.

For the spring and summer of 1894, people within Wilmette continued to debate about the issue. By the fall, another election was held with the "Wilmette Citizens Association" winning a slightly larger 54% of the vote (as opposed to the 50.4% victory in the spring), which settled the matter of independence.

***

It's peculiar that Fr. Netstraeter, whom by modern standards is considered the godfather of Wilmette, wanted to see the town annexed. We can make the assumption that Fr. Netstraeter saw the move to Evanston as beneficial to the *people* of Wilmette with lower taxes and better municipal services. Although he served on Wilmette's Board of Trustees and was a mayor himself, Fr. Netstraeter believed that annexation would be better for the residents. This suggests that he wasn't concerned with his own legacy or prestige. Despite the achievements during his lifetime, one doesn't get the impression of Fr. Netstraeter being a prideful man. Perhaps he wasn't concerned about letting Evanston take over what he built, specifically because he wanted what was best for his "flock."

Within this debate, Evanston's local high school was a major point of contention on the issue. Fr. Netstraeter was, in a sense, a teacher and principal of his own school, so it makes sense that he would want higher education available for his people. ~~The failure of Wilmette annexing to Evanston paved the way for what would become one of the United States'~~ most respected ~~schools.~~

The Creation of New Trier Township High School

Throughout the 1890s, Fr. Netstraeter had been petitioning the Archdiocese* of Chicago to assist with the creation and building of another Chicago school for "secondary education" (i.e. high school). Throughout this decade the population of Wilmette was still increasing and offered few, if any, outlets to continue education for children who finished grade school. The Archdiocese rejected his proposals, so Fr. Netstraeter decided to use his government connections to establish a new school.

Fr. Netstraeter eventually rounded together four partners, particularly Dr. Byron Stolp, who worked alongside him in the attempt to annex Wilmette to Evanston. Dr. Stolp had been active on the Wilmette School Board, making him a valuable asset in the politics in getting a secondary school started.

In 1899, a referendum to provide this secondary education was put to a vote to the Villages of Glenco, Kenilworth, Wilmette and Winnetka. Attorney Merritt Starr, a resident of Winnetka and noted for arguing cases in front of the U.S. Supreme Court, was a major advocate and influence in pushing for the new secondary school. On April 4, 1899, the villages voted

---

* The year 1880 was when the "Diocese" of Chicago was elevated to an "Archdiocese."

in favor (651 for, 369 against) of the creation of a new high school.

Over a month later, on May 19, the first board meeting took place with the five "founders" of the school, including Fr. Netstraeter. The board minutes indicate that Fr. Netstraeter suggested options be acquired on several parcels of "township" land (i.e. government property) near the railroad tracks.(3) By August, the request for $60,000 in bonds was approved and issued in December.

Over a year later, on February 4, 1901, New Trier Township High School held its first day of classes for 76 students (40 girls, 36 boys). They named the school *New Trier* in honor of the home country from where many German ancestors in the area came from.

With New Trier's founding in 1901, Fr. Netstraeter remained on the school board for the following eight years. As with the real estate endeavors, this act is bizarre by modern standards; an ordained member of a religious organization is involved with the founding of, and then participates as an active member of a *public school* board. Today this concept might be considered so taboo that it would spark widespread outcry – particularly with regards to the concept of "separation of church and state."

By the end of the century, in the mid-1990s, the fact that a Catholic priest was involved with the founding of — by then the very popular New Trier

Township High School, was glossed over. A New Trier superintendent (who shall remain anonymous) assumed the fact wrong when local historians were researching Fr. Netstraeter for an article.

The faculty and students of the first New Trier High School student body in 1901.

Chapter Eight
Wet vs. Dry

The Village of Gross Point

On March 10, 1874, two years after the incorporation of Wilmette, the new Village of Gross Point was incorporated just along the western border of Wilmette. At the time, the village was home to approximately 450 people. The boundaries rested along Ridge Road, cutting a path that placed St. Joseph's directly opposite of Gross Point's; Ridge Road was the dividing line between Wilmette and Gross Point. Due to the layout of the villages, the majority of Catholics in Gross Point were parishioners of St. Joseph's, rather than St. Peter's in Skokie four miles south. As a whole, Gross Point was relatively smaller than the neighboring Evanston, Skokie, Wilmette and Winnetka.

Beginning in the 1890s, the small village became very wealthy, very popular commercially and very controversial, despite its small size.

The Temperance Movement

The United States' trouble with alcohol started long before the signing of the Declaration of

Independence, when the consumption of alcohol was shockingly high. As early as 1790, civic leader and Declaration signer Benjamin Rush had advocated for public restraint against drinking. In 1826, the Temperance Society was formed, and by 1835, it grew to 1,500,000 members across the country. The movement to outlaw alcohol throughout the United States was not an altogether foreign idea, particularly to the forest-heavy Grosse Pointe territory when Northwestern University (just south) enacted restrictions against the sale of alcohol in 1855. While the Civil War raged between 1861 and 1865, the agenda lost its momentum, but at the end of the decade in 1869, the Prohibition Party was formed. Although this political party never gained any seats in Congress, its progressive ideas fueled the creation of the Women's Christian Temperance Union in 1873. By the following decade, Kansas was the first state to outlaw alcohol in 1881, with other small towns and counties following suit. By the turn of the century in 1900, the sale of alcohol had truly become a subject of major political contention.

 A good benchmark to understanding the gravity of the alcohol dilemma can be seen by way of the Anti-Saloon League, a lobbying group that pushed for outlawing alcohol. This organization was able to draw supporters from diverse groups across the country, including both Democrats and Republicans. Incredibly, the Anti-Saloon League found support from *both* the National Association for the Advancement of Colored People (NAACP) and the Ku Klux Klan (KKK). One of the targets of the Anti-Saloon League were German breweries, which is an example of anti-German sentiment within the Temperance Movement.

Generally speaking within the Christian faiths, the Protestants were in support of "dry," as the concept of restraint and adsention from alcohol was more in line with their Puritan roots. Catholics on the other hand were in favor of "wet," believing that the government should not dictate morality to its people.

Wet Town: The Village of Gross Point

The story of Gross Point's economy is extremely similar to the birth of a famous gambling industry in the state of Nevada. Although illegal for decades, gambling was eventually authorized by Nevada's state legislator for an outpost city called Las Vegas, and the first casino went up on Fremont Street. The neighborhood quickly realized the potential profit for local businesses, and other casinos were established. Fremont Street was the first paved street in Las Vegas and the first to receive traffic lights in 1931 – during the Great Depression.

The difference between the "old classic Vegas" Fremont Street of Las Vegas and the now humble Ridge Road of Wilmette was the era of prohibition.

Evanston was one of the first local governments to adopt the anti-alcohol mentality, particularly because it was home to Northwestern University. When Evanston was incorporated in 1863, the first act was to institute an ordinance banning alcohol within a four mile radius of the campus and the city's boundaries. Furthermore, Evanston was home to leading members of the Women's Christian Temperance Movement, making the city one of the premiere "dry" spots in the country long before it became a major political agenda.

Evanston's four mile radius restriction ended where the Village of Gross Point's property began. The small town, packed with German Catholics, was not going to adhere to the "dry" policies of Evanston, Wilmette and Winnetka. Throughout the 1870s and 1880s, Gross Point allowed the sale of alcohol and therefore attracted drinkers from nearby.

It wasn't until the 1890s that the bar business in Gross Point grew substantially, transforming the small town into one of the most economically thriving of Chicago's north shore area. Several factors played into the economic success, beginning with Northwestern's very own students who, unsurprisingly, were a major source of revenue as they often traveled the few miles required to Gross Point's saloons.

The larger breweries from downtown Chicago were also invested in the town, as they would put up the capital for the construction of the bars, however, that company's product would be the main item available at the saloon. This is no different from the modern concept of a Nike Store, an Apple Store or a Disney Store; while Nike, Apple and Disney products can be found in practically every department store across the country – those stores are exclusive for their own products. The same concept would apply to the Gross Point bars – one brand name would be the dominant beer of the given bar.

Gross Point was able to install wooden sidewalks and gas streetlights; both luxuries of the time. Although the population of Gross Point started with less than 300, by 1897 it was well over 500 residents, and opened up its own smaller public school just a mile south from St. Joseph's school.

One of the most popular images of Wilmette's history – three gentleman in one of Gross Point's bars. In the middle, Michael Loutch who was one of the area's most successful farmers and a parishioner of St. Joseph's.

John Mick was one of fourteen bars that stood along Ridge Road with *John Mick* being <u>directly</u> across the street from St. Joseph's church.

The large sign, "The Standard Bottle Beers" on the side of the building is one of four advertisements seen in this photo for *Standard Beer*. This is a perfect example of a bar being funded by a specific brand. Notice the hanging laundry (left) along the side of the building, indicating that the family lived above the bar.

As taverns became the primary source of income for Gross Point, more began opening up at the turn of the century, and each new bar made the city more controversial. The high number of saloons in Gross Point was a metaphorical slap in the face to Evanston's self-righteous view of themselves (the Women's Christian Temperance Union had moved its headquarters into Evanston in 1900). In some ways, since the consumption of alcohol became more of a "hot button" issue and the political temperature grew, the popularity of the subject was in turn fueling Gross Point's capitalistic success.

It's important to note that as more people ventured to the "wet" city, the business of prostitution was also enacted in at least some of the taverns as restrictions on the practice were less harsh than by modern standards.

The Moral Dilemma

The figure caught in the center of this local government dispute was Fr. Netstraeter, both mentally and physically. On the one hand, the German taverns were a major source of tax-free income to his parishioners. A significant portion of his real estate business was in Gross Point and Fr. Netstraeter had fared very well from this practice (again, he benefited so well from the real estate business that he never took a salary from St. Jospeh's). Hence, since Gross Point's keynote popularity was indebted to drinking, inadvertently more and more people were venturing to the area.

On the other hand, the Temperance Movement was successfully propagandizing the concept that alcohol was tearing families apart. Drinking was causing men to become lazy and/or violent, an especially disturbing sentiment for the pastor of St. Joseph's sitting in "dry" Wilmette. Directly across the street from St. Joseph's (where Gross Point's city boundaries began) there grew to be *fifteen* taverns along the other side. The folklore among St. Joseph's parishioners was that Sunday mornings saw mother and child in church while the husbands/fathers were across the street at the bars. In all seriousness this is probably a strong exaggeration or even creative fiction. Nevertheless, for a church to be placed so close to an establishment that was considered harmful to families (i.e. drunkenness, rowdiness, whoring), there was a sort of embarrassment on the part of St. Joseph's Parish.

***

If there is one topic in Fr. Netstraeter's biography that leaves more to be desired, it's this subject. Considering that Catholics were generally on the side of anti-prohibition and that German immigrants had been celebrated (or scorned) because of their breweries, it leaves one to wonder if Fr. Netstraeter was on the fence with this dilemma. Unfortunately we don't know if Fr. Netstraeter struggled with making a decision, or if he was firm in his convictions. Again, there are questions that remain unanswered: did he himself enjoy alcohol? Or was he always outwardly opposed to it? Or did he become progressively more anti-alcohol given the circumstances?

Anti-German Sentiment in the Late 1800s

It's possible that Fr. Netstraeter also struggled with prevalent anti-German sentiment within the Temperance Movement. Since the Germans owned and operated a majority of the breweries, it's no surprise that they were targets for those who sought to ban alcohol.

In fact, despite the "progressive" view of the Temperance Movement and the Women's Christian Temperance Union, the overall sentiment was one of anti-immigration. Just as the Irish were discriminated against in the mid-1800s, the Germans of the Grosse Pointe region faced prejudice and bigotry due to their brewing businesses.

As stated, the Anti-Saloon League explicitly forced closings of German breweries. Hence, it's not a far-fetched concept to wonder if Fr. Netstraeter was distraught at the obvious attacks on his own brethren. It wasn't only about alcohol; the Temperance Movement exploited the current sentiments that disliked immigrants. Though the end goal was to ban alcohol, the cause essentially allowed for continued bigotry against the Germans. Fr. Netstraeter already had financial concerns in showing any support for the Temperance Movement; the struggle to possibly "go against" his own people must have weighed heavily on his mind.

Local Government Votes
to Close the Gross Point Bars

In the era when local governments were taking the alcohol question into their own hands, the state of Illinois passed a Local Option Law in 1907. This brought the matter up to a vote within the municipal governments of Evanston, Gross Point, Kenilworth, Wilmette and Winnekta. Despite the popularity of the town, the residents of Gross Point were outnumbered and the bars were forced to close their doors in a landslide vote of 1,318 to 740; a decade before the passing of the 18th Amendment.[1]

The victorious vote to close the taverns of Gross Point was endorsed by Fr. Netstraeter.

A Visceral Reaction

Unfortunately the definitive driving force behind Fr. Netstraeter's decision to support the closing of the Gross Point bars remain unknown, although there are some valid theories: perhaps the close proximity between the taverns, (specifically the behavior of customers) and St. Joseph's school was seen as a threat? Perhaps a moral reason, in that Fr. Netstraeter didn't want his "flock" to fall victim to drunkenness and whoring. Wilmette historian, John Jacoby attributes a quote to Fr. Netstraeter's, saying that the saloons were: "a threat to the youth of the community".

To be clear, Fr. Netstraeter was endorsing something was, arguably, financially damaging to the neighborhood and possibly his parishioners. The ban of alcohol was such a catastrophic event for the Village of Gross Point that it incited violence. Despite there are no definitive records that explicitly articulate *how* the saloons were effecting St. Joseph's Parish, the blame was fixated on Fr. Netstraeter.

John Jacoby explains that some members of Gross Point were irate and took extreme action:

> A crowd tried to tear down the fence at Father Netstraeter's residence, and someone vandalized the gardens at the nearby house of his colleague, Rev. Edward Vattman. The saloonkeepers threatened to ignore the outcome of the referendum.[2]

Despite the violence, the outrage of citizens and the concerning future for Wilmette and Gross Point's relationship, it is recorded that Fr. Netstraeter remained calm when quelling the masses. Fr. Netstraeter's first biographer, Father F.R. Kalvelage, notes that the whole neighborhood was victim to "foul means of gossip by the out-of-town clientele." Yet Fr. Kalvelage points out that in the aftermath:

> Fr. Netstraeter was adamant. After much disturbance the village quieted, the scars of

the ferocious battle healed, the respect for the community had steadily mounted to rest comfortably in their attainment of domestic serenity. Once more they were united because of the exceptionally strong character of him [Fr. Netstraeter] who they reverently and respectfully acknowledged and saluted as their Father.(3)

As with most dramatic events and displays of discontent, things eventually simmered down as Fr. Netstraeter managed to earn the community's respect despite his decisions.

By 1923, the wealth of the once up-and-coming Las Vegas-esque "fun" town was dying, so Gross Point sold off the Village Hall building in order to pay the accumulating debt. The Village of Gross Point voted to annex a large portion of itself to Wilmette in January 1924, just three months shy of Fr. Netstraeter's death. He lived just long enough to see *his* Wilmette consume the neighboring village, rather than Wilmette be taken by another. Two years later in 1926, the rest of Gross Point was annexed to Wilmette, with tiny portions going to Skokie and Evanston.

Chapter Nine
An Era Ends & Another Begins
(1915 to 1924)

In 1915, George Mundelein was appointed the Archbishop of Chicago. Having served as the Auxiliary Bishop of Brooklyn for the previous six years and being of partial German descent, Archbishop Mundelein was believed to possess the necessary experience for guiding the larger and growing Archdiocese of Chicago. This same year, St. Joseph's Parish had completed a brand-new brick school building — the final structural landmark in the major construction overhaul during Fr. Netstraeter's fifty-year pastorate.

There are not many details on the relationship between Archbishop Mundelein and Fr. Netstraeter, but we can easily assume that the two did have a friendship based off of three key reasons:

***

First, there are two photographs from February 9, 1916, at Archbishop Mundelein's installation ceremony outside of Holy Name Cathedral in

Cardinal George Mundelein

downtown Chicago. In both photos, Fr. Netstraeter is in the procession with Archbishop Mundelein, directly flanking his left side. To be that close to the new Archbishop is a clear indicator that either Fr. Netstraeter had an amicable relationship with the new Archbishop – or, the more likely that Fr. Netstraeter had prominence within the Chicago Archdiocese, earning a spot that close in a major ceremony.

***

Secondly, just over a year later on September 30, 1917, Archbishop Mundelein gave the homily at Fr. Netstraeter's Golden Jubilee Mass (a celebration for Fr. Netstraeter's fifty years of priesthood). For Fr. Netstraeter to have the most distinguished figure in the Chicago Archdiocese preach at his milestone Mass is a key indicator of their connection. Archbishop Mundelein's sermon highlighted the quantity of years Fr. Netstraeter spent at St. Joseph's, his rebuilding of the once frail parish and the overall legacy of his work. When the homily was preached, Fr. Netstraeter was currently in his forty-fifth year as pastor of St. Joseph's, and Archbishop Mundelein speaks of Fr. Netstraeter's legacy with the same amazement that future generations have remembered him for. Furthermore, it's clear that the 76-year-old pastor showed no signs of slowing down. The full text of Mundelein's homily was recorded as follows:

> Today I come here as the head of the diocese to take part in the joy and festivity that is felt in this parish from end to end, among young and old, rich and poor, Catholic and non-Catholic, because the pastor here has completed the golden circle of his priestly years, because Father Netstraeter has served God and ministered to a man for a half century, and because nearly all of that time was spent in this place. It is rather in the capacity of spokesman that I am here this morning—to express your appreciation of the many kindnesses he has shown you during the years he has been in your midst; the affection that is in your hearts for one who has been your spiritual father for so long; the gratitude you feel to the priest of the Most High who has ministered to three generations of the people of this town.
>
> We of a younger generation are apt to forget how arduous were the labors, how many were the sacrifices, how great was the toil of those early missionaries of this

diocese. The distances were great, the conveniences were few, the faithful were scattered in those days. The jubilarian of today is one of the links that bind us of the present to the missionaries of that early day. He suffered privations with them and God has granted him to help reap the fruits of their labors with us. He helped to sow the seed of God's word with them, but few, pitifully few, have survived to gather in the great harvest with us, although the crowded churches, the well-filled schools, the flourishing institutions are largely the results of their work.

And so this morning his younger brethren of the clergy have come here together with his people, that kneeling with him at this altar, where he has so long ministered, they might thank Almighty God for having given Father Netstraeter the gift to serve Him as His priest for a half century, for having left him here in this place for more than two score years, to benefit them with his priestly work and edify them with his priestly life. Usually a Golden Jubilee has a tinge of sadness. It seems like a golden sunset, the end of a perfect day, almost like a solemn farewell, when everybody is outwardly smiling but inwardly hiding his tears. But not so today. No one can look at the clear skin and the quick bright eye of our youthful septuagenarian and not recognize that after all there is a great deal of truth in the saying that a man is only as old as he looks and surely not a day older than he feels.

So, confidently I offer my good wishes to Father Netstraeter this morning, praying that the Lord may spare him for many years; that each year may treat him more kindly than its predecessor, make him more acceptable to his Master and dearer to his people, make him more revered among the clergy and beloved by the laity; that the years may pass for him quickly and happily until another jubilee day twenty-five years hence, when the golden leaves of his priestly crown of today will have become diamond-studded with the passage of time.[1]

We don't know the tone in which Archbishop Mundelein spoke the last lines hinting at another twenty-five years of Fr. Netstraeter's life, although we can safely assume it was in jest. Yet it gives further indication that Fr. Netstraeter remained vital in his 70s.

***

The third and most prominent sign of their friendship are the events that transpired over a decade *after* Fr. Netstraeter's death (detailed in Part III). We can safely assume that Mundelein had a personal stake in defending Fr. Netstraeter's family name from a young man, who was at this time, currently fighting in World War I.

On the very day that Archbishop Mundelein gave his homily at St. Joseph's celebrating Fr. Netstraeter golden jubilee, a young "gefreiter" (German for "Lance Corporal") named Adolf Hitler was just beginning a half month furlough from the military in Berlin to travel the city and study the museums. These three: Netstraeter, Mundelein and Hitler, would cross paths in exactly 21 year's time over the ad hoc phrase, "house painter of Berlin."

St. Mary of the Lake Seminary

Archbishop Mundelein had been making great strides in the Catholic communities of Chicago. One of his key aspirations was to reopen St. Mary of the Lake Seminary; the school that Bishop Quarter had closed in 1866 due to financial difficulties. Archbishop Mundelein began plans in 1921, opening the school's doors under the title of St. Mary's College.

In 1924, exactly two weeks before Fr. Netstraeter died, Mundelein was named "Cardinal" by Pope Pius XI, thus making Chicago the first diocese in the Midwest to have a Cardinal. To be elevated to the position of Cardinal is to become a leading and authoritative figure in more than Catholicism – the world religious as well. For example, only a Cardinal can vote for Pope.(2)

It was not until 1926, two years after Fr. Netstraeter's death, that Cardinal Mundelein officially reopened the Seminary under the name St. Mary of the Lake. It was used as the site for that year's International Eucharistic Congress, a four-day event that drew nearly 1 million people to its concluding Mass at St. Mary of the Lake; today, this location is commonly known as Mundelein Seminary.

Unbeknownst to all at the time, Fr. Netstraeter, though he died in 1924, plays into the establishment of St. Mary of the Lake in a substantial way.

The Last Year

The vitality that Archbishop Mundelein praised Fr. Netstraeter for would remain for another six years. By 1923, Fr. Netstraeter had tallied *fifty-one years* as pastor of St. Joseph's Parish in Wilmette.

Although long tenures were more common in this era, five decades was a stretch; arguably the longest span for any priest or minister to accomplish. Fr. Netstraeter announced his retirement in 1923, and in July, Father John Neumann took over St. Joseph's as pastor.

Fr. Netstraeter standing outside of the rectory; this is presumed to be the last photograph of him.

Pastors did not generally retire in this era, so the fact that Fr. Netstraeter chose to step away before his death was perhaps a sign that his health was failing.

Fr. Netstraeter died Monday, April 7, 1924, of a cerebral hemorrhage. The details surrounding his death are not known, however Fr. Netstraeter's death certificate indicates arteriosclerosis as a secondary cause of death. Although no autopsy was performed, we can safely assume a blood clot resulted in a stroke. His funeral took place Thursday, April 10 at 10:00a.m. His passing was a cover story of the local *Wilmette Life* which noted Fr. Netstraeter's death with the following:

> The pastor of St. Joseph's was, without doubt, one of the most prominent ecclesiastics in this part of the United States. He was a zealous churchman and labored assiduously for the welfare not only of his own parishioners but also of the whole community. His was an honored life, full of good deeds and a blessing to a multitude.[3]

The Last Will & Testament

To accurately judge the success of Fr. Netstraeter's real estate business, one can look to what he gave back to his home, St. Joseph's – the parish he pastored and never took a salary from.

In his will, Fr. Netstraeter directed that the sum of his estate, totaling $300,000, be used for the construction of a brand-new church. From 1924 to the late 2010s, the inflation on that amount of money would be equivalent to *$4 million dollars*, evidence that this Catholic priest was extremely wealthy. Aside from collected stories of his monetary shrewdness, there was never any recording of Fr. Netstraeter being lavishly wealthy – however it would explain why in the fifty-one years of his pastorate, St. Joseph's never encountered any financial scares similar to its early years, or even other Catholic parishes in general.

Yet Fr. Netstraeter wanted his acquired real estate funds funneled right back into his life's calling: Catholicism.

As St. Joseph's parishioners were unprepared for this gift, Fr. Netstraeter's will directed Cardinal Mundelein to oversee the large sum of money for five years until it was ready to be used for a new church. When there were still no building plans two years after his death, Cardinal Mundelein borrowed the full sum of Fr. Netstraeter's estate to cover expenses for the revival of St. Mary of the Lake Seminary.

There is no concern that Cardinal Mundelein was going to keep ("steal") the $300,000 inside of the Seminary's funds indefinitely. The most likely reason, however, that the money remained in the Seminary's hands for so long is the Great Depression which started in 1929. Additionally, we can safely assume that St. Joseph's parish was not prepared to facilitate the building of a brand-new church as they were in the early process of revitalizing the school when Fr. Netstraeter died.

Hence, Fr. Netstraeter's money would not be "returned" until 1938, fourteen years after his death. Even in the late 1930s, his will was executed sooner than anticipated. *No one* foresaw that the political fanatic in Munich, who was gaining minor attention in the American press, and who was recently sent to prison for a failed overthrow of the government, was going play a role in this story.

An expert from Fr. Netstraeter's will that directs "the Most Rev. George W. Mundelein" to oversee usage of the money.

Part III

Chapter Ten
Catholicism vs. National Socialism
(1907 to 1937)

An Angry Aspiring Artist

Adolf Hitler first traveled to Vienna in September 1907 to take the entrance exam for the Academy of Fine Arts, but he failed on the final round of tests.(1) The following year, Hitler moved to Vienna with a friend, August Kubizek, who had passed the entrance exam for the Academy. By the following September, Hitler applied to the school again, but was not even invited to take the entrance exam. The second rejection spurred an outrage as recalled by Kubizek:

> "This Academy!" Hitler yelled. "Nothing but a pack of cramped, old, outmoded servants of the state, clueless bureaucrats, stupid creations of the civil service! The whole academy should be dynamited!" His face was pale, his lips were pressed so tightly together that they went white. His

eyes were glowing. How uncanny his eyes were! As if all the hatred of which he was capable were burning in those eyes. (2)

This outburst was one of the first documented incidents of Hitler's anger whenever he was slighted. The angry outbursts would become more common in future years.

Due to his failure to get into the Academy, Hitler moved out and rented a new apartment in November of 1908. By August of 1909 he had moved again, into cheaper quarters, but eventually found himself a vagrant — either sleeping on the street or in a men's shelter. During this time, Hitler took on menial construction jobs, one of which *may have been* wallpaper hanging.

At 20, Hitler befriended a contemporary from the men's shelter named Reinhold Hanisch, and the two started working together, selling Hitler's quaint postcard paintings. They evidently had success from doing this, as the two were able to move out of the men's shelter in February 1910. Yet by August, the two had a falling out when Hitler discovered (and subsequently reported to the police) that Hanisch was hiding funds from the sales. Hitler would continue finding clients to buy his paintings — the most prominent being a Jewish-owned framing and art shop.

For the next three years, Hitler would continue to dabble in this bohemian lifestyle: spending his days in café's, venturing out into the countryside to paint landscapes, or staying in the city to paint landmarks. Some witnesses from around this time note there were occasionally short-lived heated political rants from the young artist. Hitler moved to Munich in May 1913, after being of age to receive his deceased father's inheritance.(3)

In August 1914, Hitler enlisted to fight in World War I, essentially ending his career as a watercolor artist.

"Vienna State Opera House," 1912. Given his love for Richard Wagner's operas, this was one of Hitler's favorite places to visit. It's not surprising he did such a detailed painting of it.

"Outskirts of a town with bridge and figures," 1909.

"The Courtyard of the Old Residency in Munich," 1914.

Catholicism vs. National Socialism 159

"Mother Mary with the Holy Child Jesus Christ," 1913.

"House at a Lake with Mountains," 1910.

After World War I: Hitler's Political Rise

Although raised Catholic (there is no indication if Hitler's family were devout Catholics or not), it's after World War I where aspects of Hitler's biography begins to contrast Catholicism.

***

As a veteran of World War I, Hitler was distraught by Germany's loss on November 10, 1918. Writing in his autobiography *Mein Kampf*, Hitler was in the hospital recovering from a mustard gas attack when the chaplain announced the news of the German surrender. It brought him to tears:

> Everything went black...I felt and stumbled my way back to my sickbed and buried my burning head in my blanket and pillow... Everything had been in vain... Had everything happened only so that a band of criminals could get their hands on our fatherland?...In the nights that followed, my hatred grew, my hatred for those responsible for this deed. (4)

A year later, Hitler joined the German Workers' Party, seeing that the political party was based in ideas of Nationalism (pro-Germany), anti-communism (enemies of Germany), and anti-Semitism (as the Jews were blamed for Germany's economic downturn). In 1920, the German Workers' Party rebranded itself as the

National Socialist German Workers' Party, which in German means: *Nationalsozialistische Deutsche Arbeiterpartei* (the word "Nazi" derives from the first word, "Nationalsozialist").[5]

In short order, Hitler rose through the ranks to become the Nazi party's leader. His charisma and passionate speeches gave him an edge above other members.[6] Leaders of the political movement knew that they relied heavily on Hitler's tactics and enthusiasm.

Historian A.N. Wilson makes the observation that Hitler's timing was providential because he emerged at a time when the *spoken word* was taking precedence over the *written word*. Wilson writes, "Hitler belonged to the oral future, the future which contained Walt Disney, television and cinema."[7]

Hitler engraved his personal ideology into the Nazi party and orchestrated the political machine to become a cultural influence. In the process, one major blunder worked out in the Nazis' favor: Hitler served ten months in prison for treason after the Nazi party attempted to overthrow the Bavarian government in 1923. Known as the Munich Beer Hall Putsch, this unsuccessful coup d'état gave Hitler national and some global attention. The Nazis learned from the Putsch's failure that a strictly violent revolution was not the way to achieve power; rather, they would have to work from a social activist angle. In prison, Hitler wrote *Mein*

Adolf Hitler

Kampf (in English, "My Struggle"), which explicitly lays out his anti-Semitic views, intermixed with his Christian background. When the Nazis began to achieve *real* political power in the 1930s, Hitler's benevolence to the Catholic Church changed once its leaders began displaying political opposition.

***

Hitler's misunderstanding of Catholicism relates to his lust for power. Again, A.N. Wilson describes it best when explaining that Hitler saw Christianity as a "success" because it refused to change dogma, and that he admired the "discipline" the Church asked of its followers:

> Hitler hated Catholicism and in time came to persecute it. But he learnt much from watching its system of power. He told Heinrich Himmler how much he had admired, as a youth, the way in which the Pope and his henchmen had put down Modernism in 1905-6. He admired the dedication of its celibate clergy. He admired, too, the fact that it was classless.

He admired its unchanging teachings. He admired its ability to intrude and snoop into private lives. He admired its lack of kindness. Above all, he admired its organizational skills. (8)

It is important to note that the Catholic Church, as an institution managed by humans, has "lacked kindness" and "intruded" throughout history. However, these errors have often been ridiculed and denounced by future generations.

Hitler Youth

In 1926, the Nazis formed a militant youth group called *Hitler Youth: League of German Worker Youth*. This new organization had a swift integration into the paramilitary branch of the Nazi party, which as the name suggests, emphasized military training. Youth groups were extremely popular for morale in post-World War I Germany, and most of them were based in religion or politics — not military action (at least not at first). *Hitler Youth* was therefore a radical change in how youth groups operated, and its numbers grew quickly after its inception.*

The Nazi Party was one of many vying for power in the late 1920s, but their influence grew

---

* By the time the Nazis had gained majority power in 1933, the number of kids enrolled in *Hitler Youth* was well over 2 million.

substantially in thanks to the Great Depression. Hitler and his cohorts certainly had public appeal and a flourishing youth group, but their support was still weak compared to other, more traditional nationalist parties. However, when the Great Depression hit Germany in 1930, Hitler blamed the poverty and unemployment on Jewish and Bolshevik financiers. He appealed to the middle class and toned down his blatant anti-Semitism just enough to gain widespread popularity. In 1933, Hitler was elected as the Chancellor of Germany in the Reichstag elections. The Nazi party had won 37.4% of the vote, making it Germany's largest political party. In the following years, Hitler's regime would overcome the Depression faster than any of the other more advanced industrial nations. (9)

Joseph Goebbels congratulating a 16-year-old member of *Hitler Youth* for his military commitment.

Between January 1933 and September 1939, Hitler's master plan went into effect and within the six-year timespan:
- Hitler combined the roles of Chancellor and President to become an overlord.
- The Gestapo (i.e. secret police) was formed, which oversaw local governments.
- All other political parties and their propaganda were banned.
- Trade unions were banned.
- Germany withdrew from the League of Nations.
- The army was expanded.
- It became mandatory that all boys join *Hitler Youth*.
- And of course, Hitler set the stage for the Axis alliance with Italy and Japan. Specifically with Benito Mussolini of Italy, Hitler's plan was to dominate all of Europe through forceful land acquisition; the conquering of the other nations.

World War II wouldn't "officially" begin until September 1, 1939, when Nazi Germany invaded and occupied of Poland.

The German Catholic Youth

As the Nazis grew in power and influence throughout the 1930s, German Catholics grew wary of *Hitler Youth* influencing their children in ways that contradicted Catholic teaching. Despite the ideals that the Nazis claimed to uphold, the differences in community living were explicit. Although the Nazi's nationalistic views promoted "unity," some Catholics saw it as a sham since the Nazi officials were steadfast in keeping the kids of the *Hitler Youth* (typically boys) separate from Catholic churches.

The leaders of the Nazi party viewed the Roman Catholic Church as a threat to its political ideology, especially when concerning the youth. The Catholic milieu in Germany (i.e. parishes, schools, youth groups) was embedded in all aspects of the children's upbringing, building a social environment that formed them as they headed into the larger society. The Catholic Church in 1930s Germany was steeped in deep tradition, whereas *Hitler Youth*, with their mandatory labor services, infused a negative change: a cultural clash arose between raising children in traditional, routine and family based principles vs. raising children in isolated secular groups.

The Roman Catholic Church walked the tightrope between loyalty and disobedience towards the Nazis for several years, yet the German Catholic youth was outspoken regarding their dissatisfaction with the Nazi rule.[*] In retaliation to the Nazis' pressure on

---

[*] Perhaps one of the best examples of this outspokenness would be the bishop of Münster, (the city where Father Netstraeter attended seminary), Bishop Clemens August Graf von Galen. A prolific example

Catholicism, processions, pilgrimages to holy sites, and other forms of public worship surged in frequency among the youth. This drew other Catholic adults from neighboring provinces and dioceses, despite the fear of censorship. (10)

***

This increase of public religious practices parallels Fr. Fortmann and the German settlers from the Grosse Pointe territory nearly a hundred years previous. We see once again that respect for the sacred draws dedicated congregants.

Nazis and the Vatican

The Nazis were hesitant in light of the church's renewed vigilance. In July 1933, six months after the Nazis became the majority in Germany, the Vatican signed a Concordat with the Third Reich securing the Catholic Church's rights to operate in Germany, as long as bishops acted within German law. As happened countless times throughout Hitler's regime, the Nazis were the first to breach contract by restricting displays of public worship.

However, because of the Concordat, the Nazis knew better than to outrightly persecute the Catholic

---

of Nazi resistance, Bishop von Galen originally hoped that Hitler's regime would return pride, respect and, perhaps, a spiritual devotion to the German people. Yet Bishop von Clemens was quick to denounce Nazism once the persecution of Catholics began.

Joseph Goebbels (left), Adolf Hitler (center) and Bishop Cesare Orsenigo (right) in April 1933.

church the same way they had Jews. Catholic Mass was not banned (at least not for several years), but was confined to indoor spaces. Nevertheless, the Masses were often filled to maximum capacity, and in time, evolved into pseudo-protests against the Nazi government.

Clashing Ideologies

The simmering anxiety grew to a boil following a Christ the King celebration in October 1934. At least twenty-five cities held separate demonstrations; the Cologne Cathedral in particular had 20,000 young people, with an additional 2,000 to 3,000 more outside. It was evident that the German Catholic people desired religious freedom over socialism. [11]

The Nazis, watchful of any and all potential opposition, realized this sentiment within the German Catholic community and were concerned that the Catholic Church would divert away from National Socialism. In other words, a "traditional" church would encourage Christian unity, i.e. a unity welcoming to other races and creeds.

The Nazis chose to combat this ideology by exploiting the unemployment dilemma. *Hitler Youth* created a little-known program called *The Land Year*, which sought to engage children (both genders, but primarily girls) in labor centric activities.

For *The Land Year*, the Nazis picked young people out of their tight-knit comfortable parish environments and transported them to camps where there was not a hint of religion. Prior to leaving for *The Land Year*, priests and parents would do their best to prepare the children and keep in contact — however, once on camp site, priests were banned and religious publications were confiscated.

This "cultural" displacement of young German Catholics brought about the term, the "Wandering Church." Although these kids were sheltered from direct Nazi ideology, they were still separated from Catholic centric environments.

Upon these children's return home from *The Land Year*, Catholic officials did their best to reinstate a sense of religious unity among these "Wandering Church" kids. The Catholic Church, knowing it was under attack, saw *The Land Year*'s youth labor service camps as an ideological battlegrounds.

The Night of the Long Knives

Originally, Hitler had only wished to combat Catholicism politically, but continuous resistance and outcry from the Church and its members caused priorities to sway. Eventually priests and clergy had no choice but to denounce Hitler and Nazism as a whole; it wasn't enough to merely criticize *parts* of the ideology.

Between June 30 to July 2, 1934, Hitler carried out a series of executions where Nazi special unit officers murdered prominent public opponents of National Socialism to solidify a stronger hold on the German nation. Though the official list released by the Nazi-controlled government state that 77 people were murdered, many believe that over 100 people lost their lives at the hands of the Gestapo during the purge.

In the wake of "The Night of the Long Knives," priests and clergy were systematically arrested and sent to concentration camps. Catholic schools and churches were closed, and teaching the faith was criminalized.

Joseph Goebbels vs. Pope Pius XII

Hitler's minister of propaganda, Joseph Goebbels, was at the frontlines of attacking Catholicism. Goebbels, aware of the Judaic foundations of Christianity, sought to replace the faith with National Socialism, with the Führer as a Christ-like savior.

In March 1937, Pope Pius XII published the encyclical, *With Burning Concern*. Nazi Historian Anthony Read describes Pius XII's letter as:

> an obvious attack on the Nazi regime...[it] condemned those who worshipped the

idols of race, people, state, or the holders of state power. (12)

Goebbels retaliated by banning Catholic publications that printed *With Burning Concern*, but Hitler wanted more to be done. Goebbels obliged.

Fabricated Sex Scandals

By the late 1930s, Goebbels had asserted himself as a cultural watchdog, believing himself to be a "defender of morality," jumping on lewd sex crimes and scandals within the Catholic clergy to exploit the church. For example, Goebbels targeted the *Brothers of Charity*, a Franciscan organization, smearing them as dangerous pedophiles and homosexuals (same-sex relations were illegal at the time). Of the 500 Franciscan friars living in Germany, over half of them were arrested. Goebbels arranged to have all German newspapers publish uncensored and graphic reports of the Nazis' findings to create further public distrust within the Catholic church. (13)

The majority of the world, particularly Catholics, saw past these obvious (and conveniently timed) scandals in the German church. Among the critics calling out Nazi Germany was Chicago's Cardinal, George Mundelein.

Chapter Eleven
A Battle of Words
(1937)

The *Austrian Paper Hanger* speech

On May 18, 1937, just two months after Pope Pius XII's formal denouncement of the Nazi regime, Cardinal Mundelein gave a speech to 500 priests at Quigley Seminary in downtown Chicago. The Cardinal addressed the desensitization of Germany as a warning of dangerous ideologies:

> Perhaps you will ask how it is that a nation of sixty-million intelligent people will submit in fear and servitude to an alien, an Austrian paper hanger, and a poor one at that, and a few associates like [Joseph] Goebbels and [Hermann] Goering, who dictate every move of the people's lives? (1)

The "Austrian paper hanger" whom Mundelein referred to was Adolf Hitler, referencing his former profession as a wallpaper hanger, but also an indirect derogatory comment about Hitler's failure as a professional watercolor artist. The insult was a double entendre: the physical job of applying wallpaper requires no creativity; it is basic and simple. Furthermore, Mundelein implied Hitler was delusional to think that that the global audience would believe these false scandals against the German clergy.

As a prominent figure of the Catholic church, Cardinal Mundelein's speech didn't go unnoticed. While many religious and political leaders in the United States supported Mundelein's remarks, some feared the slight would spur a greater rift between German-American relations. The U.S.-German ambassador, Hans H. Dieckoff, expressed his concerns:

> The Germany Embassy at Washington made energetic representations in the State Department on account of the silly and tactless insults to the Fuhrer [Hitler] and Reichsfuehrer [Goebbels] by Chicago Cardinal Mundelein. (2)

Dieckoff and Goebbels attempted to organize protests in Germany over Cardinal Mundelein's remarks, but to little avail. They then appealed to the Holy See in Rome, trying to get the Chicago Cardinal reprimanded, yet the prelates (bishops and other ecclesial dignitaries) replied that Cardinal Mundelein could speak his mind on foreign affairs.

The Vatican's dismissal of Cardinal Mundelein's words emphasized that the Catholic

Church had seen past Goebbels and Hitler's ruse. Furthermore, it came at a time when the tide in opinion was shifting across the globe: nations were beginning to see Nazi Germany as the oppressive government that it was.

President Franklin D. Roosevelt (left) and Cardinal Mundelein (right). The writing in the middle was Cardinal Mundelein's note to FDR.

Hitler, known for his untimely public outbursts*(3), was not going to ignore the insult,

---

* In the aftermath of the Munich Beer Hall Putsch, Hitler remained in hiding at a safe house with a dislocated shoulder. During this time Hitler was calm, but when it was announced that the police knew his whereabouts, Hitler was reported to have "completely lost his nerve,"

especially as it grew in front of a global audience and was compelled to retaliate.(4)

Fr. Netstraeter's Will & Testament

No aspect of Fr. Netstraeter's biography is more convoluted than how his last will was executed, and how his final building, St. Joseph's church, came into being. To date, there remains an uneasy amount of speculation as to how *exactly* St. Joseph's church was funded.

There are few definitive facts that *need* to be highlighted first:

1. Fr. Netstraeter died in April, 1924.

2. Fr. Netstraeter's last will and testament bequeathed $300,000 to St. Joseph's Parish in Wilmette, Illinois *specifically* for the construction of a new church edifice.

3. Through inflation, $300,000 in the 1920s would be equivalent to approximately $4-million in the 2010s.

4. In 1926, three years after his death, Cardinal Mundelein borrowed this bequeathed money to finance the re-opening of St. Mary of the Lake Seminary.

---

and flew into a rage, yelling "Now all is lost! No use going on!" while taking his pistol and nearly committing suicide.

5. By the year 1937, *fourteen years after* his death, that $300,000 sum had yet to be used for the construction of a new church. Therefore, Fr. Netstraeter's last will and testament had *not* been executed.

***

There are *three* different versions of how Fr. Netstraeter's will was executed and used to construct St. Joseph's Church in 1938 & 1939. What makes this matter more complicated is that there are contradictions between the three stories. After careful review, we believe that all three are *likely* based in truth, but the details got fuddled overtime thanks to creative fiction on the part of parish and Wilmette folklore.

First Version: The Wealthy Aunt

In the late 1800s or early 1900s, Fr. Netstraeter's aunt from Trier, Germany, died leaving him a large sum of money in *her* last will. Since she was living in Germany, her will had to be probated in her home country (i.e. Germany) before the money could be transferred to someone in the United States. This resulted in the money being tied up in the German probate system for many years. One could understand that the German government did not want a large sum of money leaving their country for any number of reasons.

The "legend" is that when Hitler became chancellor of Germany in 1933, he (or someone in his cabinet) was aware of this large sum of money awaiting transfer to the United States. Of course, Hitler would have opposed a transfer of "German money" to the United States, and was incented to keep the funds in German possession after Cardinal Mundelein's public attack.

The Wealthy Aunt: Fact or Fiction?

What makes this story difficult is that the aunt's name and date of death remains unknown. Specifically, not knowing her date of death opens up the extremely confusing possibility of alternate timelines. If the aunt's bequest was made in the 1880s, the German government would certainly *not* want money going to a Catholic priest.[*] If the bequest was during the World War I years (late 1910s) or immediately following (1920s) the German government would desperately want to hold on to the funds for the war effort.[†]

The "wealthy aunt" version offers more questions than answers: was Fr. Netstraeter a legal

---

[*] The 1880s era in Germany was the time of Kulturkampf, when chancellor Otto von Bismarck enacted sanctions against the Catholic Church and tried to subject the Church to state control.

[†] The Treaty of Versailles in 1919 forced Germany to pay war reparations. This was made increasingly hard due to the Great Depression which followed.

citizen of the United States at the time, therefore making the transfer of money even tougher? Was his inheritance the entire sum of $300,000? Was this money received before his death in 1923, or did he simply receive notice? Were the German courts trying to claim the sum *back* instead of blocking its transfer *to* the United States?

It is fair to assume there's *some* truth to this story; clearly Franz and William had the financial capacity to immigrate to the United States. Fr. Netstraeter had money to kick-start his real estate business and seemed to remain independently wealthy throughout his life. There likely could have been an aunt (or family member) who bequeathed money to him, however, no proof has arisen connecting a wealthy aunt to the construction of St. Joseph's Church.

The Second Version: Fr. Netstraeter's Heirs

Fr. Netstraeter's mother, Maria Schulte, had been married previously — specifically before marrying Franz Netstraeter. Maria had two children from the previous marriage which means that Fr. Netstraeter had two half-siblings.

When Franz and William immigrated to American in 1867, his half-siblings remained in Germany. These two half-siblings grew up and had children of their own; they are believed to have died before Fr. Netstraeter did.

According to Wilmette historian, John Jacoby, Fr. Netstraeter's last will had a stipulation attached to it indicating that: the parishioners of St. Joseph's needed to raise additional money to build the church within five years after Netstraeter's death. This means that the $300,000 was not enough to build a new church. Five years after Fr. Netstraeter's death (circa 1929), St. Joseph's managed to raise an additional $180,000 for the building of a new church.

It was around this time that Fr. Netstraeter's heirs entered the picture, claiming that his will was invalid because the language was "vague, indefinite, and uncertain".[4] Jacoby also points out that these family members also claimed that Fr. Netstraeter wasn't of sound mind when he wrote the will. Jacoby's history expands on the controversy explaining that:

> The latter contention was ridiculous. Witness Peter Wagner testified, "Why, the week before he [Netstraeter] died, I took him down to the election; we talked about the election and he was as good as anybody could expect. I had no idea he was sick at all."[5]

The facts support Peter Wagner's testimony, as Fr. Netstraeter's listed cause of death was a cerebral hemorrhage, likely due to a stroke. Fr. Netstraeter's death was rather sudden; there was no indication that he was becoming senile, suffering from dementia or otherwise lacking a "sound mind."

The legal battle between St. Joseph's Parish and the heirs of Fr. Netstraeter was carried out through three court proceedings: the first challenge supposedly coming from a granddaughter of one of the half-siblings. She had come to America from Germany in the early 1920s and worked as a maid in the St. Joseph rectory. Shortly after Fr. Netstraeter's death, she was the first to claim that he wasn't of sound mind when he died, and fought for the inheritance on her own behalf and on the behalf of nine relatives still in Germany. This challenge was dismissed from court, as was the second.

The third challenge went forward on the basis that Fr. Netstraeter's bequest was unclear and indefinite. The third challenge was filed in 1928 and settled in 1931, which means that Cardinal Mundelein and the executor of Fr. Netstraeter's will, both decided that there was just enough doubt regarding the bequest's clarity. The heirs obtained $30,000 – 10 percent of Fr. Netstraeter's estate – by withdrawing the case from court.

Fr. Netstraeter's Heirs: Fact or Fiction?

This version of this story is backed up with historical documentation, however it doesn't offer answers to Cardinal Mundelein's urgency to build St. Joseph's church in 1937.

Given that the Netstraeter heirs third and final challenge was settled out of court in 1931, six years before Cardinal Mundelein's controversial speech, this version dismisses Hitler's seeking revenge (the third version) as an unauthenticated legend. This second version also claims that the case was settled out of court, (which also differs from the third version involving St. Joseph's pastor, Fr. Neumann).

According to this story, St. Joseph's raised $180,000 by 1929, within five years of Fr. Netstraeter's death. Why would the Archdiocese wait for nearly a decade before constructing the new church? Though Cardinal Mundelein borrowed the entire sum to reopen St. Mary of the Lake Seminary in 1926, by 1931, when the case was settled out of court, how was the money was supposedly back in the Archdiocese's hands?

Third Version: Nazi-Orchestrated Lawsuit

The most popular version still has a few loose ends and arguably outlandish claims, yet has a consistent narrative that fits how historical events unfolded.

In August 1937, three months after Cardinal Mundelein's "paper hanger" speech, a lawsuit was filed against Father John Neumann from a German family claiming to be relatives of the late Fr. Netstraeter. This random lawsuit, from a family no one was aware of,

A Battle of Words 183

argued that the estate of Fr. Netstraeter, specifically the $300,000, was rightfully due to them.

Speculation quickly pointed to the Nazis since the lawsuit appeared from thin air. An unexpected lawsuit from a "family" in Nazi controlled Germany, specifically against a German parish within the Archdiocese of Chicago? Two organizations in a public tête-à-tête? The concept fits the Nazi playbook: just as Hitler operated in Germany, finding scandal to turn people against the Church, he sought a reason to avenge himself after Mundelein's insult.

Swearing revenge, Hitler himself (or through Joseph Goebbels) directed his Nazi agents to go to Chicago and find scandal. When in the U.S., the Nazis uncovered Fr. Netstraeter's will, discovering that it *had not* formally been executed — meaning that the $300,000 was technically unused. As the story goes, the Nazis convinced a German family to press charges, under the false claim that they were relatives of Fr. Netstraeter.

Details of how Hitler or the Nazis discovered the existence of Fr. Netstraeter's will are vague. However, given the lack of details about Fr. Netstraeter's youth, the biographical "plot holes" were easy to fill for malicious purpose.

There were three separate court hearings: the case debuted in trial court, made its way to appellate court, and then back to trial court. As the legal battle went on, Fr. Neumann's council suggested he accept an offer of settlement, which he refused. It took another four months until the Circuit Court of Cook County determined that the will's proper place was in the Archdiocese's hands.

The Vatican was made aware of the lawsuit, and upon hearing that Fr. Netstraeter's intent for the $300,000 was to build a new church, Pope Pius XII instructed Cardinal Mundelein to immediately begin construction.

Nazi Orchestrated Lawsuit: Fact or Fiction?

The story makes the most sense, but lacks the evidence to back up its more colorful claims. The idea that Nazi spies infiltrated either St. Joseph's or the Archdiocese of Chicago is a tad far-fetched. Exactly where could they have discovered the existence of Fr. Netstraeter's will, let alone the understanding that it had not been executed yet?

On the other hand, this story first appears in 1956, whereas the other versions were only recently uncovered in the 1990s at the earliest. Additionally, the "Nazi spy" lore could be explained through the German National Banks located in Chicago during the 1930s, and somehow the details of Fr. Netstraeter's will was found though those channels.

Additionally, Cardinal Mundelein could not have spent $300,000 in the late-1930s without the

Vatican's knowledge. Whether he was given "direct orders" from the Pope or not, the Vatican was certainly aware of Cardinal Mundelein's quick rush to build St. Joseph's new church.

Verdict

As we said in the very beginning, we hope that this book will usher out material that we were unable to uncover. In researching the truthfulness of these stories, we reached out to many experts and record offices. Many of these sources were uncooperative, which is why we are left to speculate the intricate details.

Assuming the old additive "the truth is somewhere in the middle", our unproven theory is as follows:

1. *If* this wealthy aunt *did* exist and *did* leave money for her nephew, she was likely responsible for the capital that Fr. Netstraeter used for his real estate career. Note that Fr. Netstraeter never took a salary from St. Joseph's, which indicates that he was independently wealthy.

2. The off-spring of the half siblings *did* most likely attempt to gain inheritance (or a portion thereof) of their wealthy half-uncle in the late 1920s or early 1930s.

3. This legal dispute between the Netstraeter heirs and St. Joseph's *was* in fact discovered by Hitler,

or Goebbels, or the Nazis after the legalities were settled. However, they attempted to exploit the situation in the summer of 1937 to harass Cardinal Mundelein.

Chapter Twelve
"Put the Money into Brick"
(1937 to 1939)

Although Cardinal Mundelein had borrowed the sum of Fr. Netstraeter's will for St. Mary of the Lake, he was likely keeping the funds incubated within the Seminary's bank(s) until the time was appropriate for St. Joseph's in Wilmette to construct a new church. Given the unusual circumstances, Cardinal Mundelein quickly had the $300,000 available shortly after the legalities were settled.

Cardinal Mundelein turned to his confidant, Joseph McCarthy, his "personal architect" (McCarthy is credited as the unofficial master builder of the Archdiocese.[1] Plans for St. Joseph's were hastily drawn up and ground was broken on the site of the new church in April 1938. At the direction of Cardinal Mundelein, McCarthy was instructed to "Put the money into brick,"* so that in the event of another leery claim being made on the $300,000, Fr. Netstraeter's will would have been formally executed to the furthest degree. The "put the

---

* This quote is most likely paraphrased.

money into brick" line was an implication that brick and mortar was something that Hitler couldn't exactly build tanks with.

The church went into construction across the street (Lake Avenue), adjacent to the new rectory. McCarthy elected for a Romanesque style with the nave of the church stretching upward. The white crescent arches all along the center aisle of the church would be "colored in" with the light from stained glass windows throughout the day as the sun rises and sets. The windows consisted primarily of blues with hints of red, making for a purple sunlit hue throughout the day.

The interior ceiling was outlined with wood; the lumber-based skeleton itself was tattooed with red and green markings resembling the Native Americans (although most would be painted over sometime in the 1980s). The sanctuary of the church features a white marble depiction of Jesus' crucifixion, the traditional centerpiece in most Catholic churches. The high altar displays the four authors of the New Testament: Saint Matthew, Saint Mark, Saint Luke and Saint John – two on each side of the golden tabernacle.

Many architectural enthusiasts have devoted studies to the current St. Joseph's in Wilmette, given it was one of Joseph McCarthy's quickest constructions, completed on a mammoth scale. The building nods to the era; the pews are bookended with triangles, giving off a subtle Radio City Music Hall vibe, popular of the era.

The bell tower is *technically* the highest point in the Village of Wilmette; the famous Baha'i Temple along Wilmette's lakefront is taller, yet it rests on the lower half of the ridge that runs through Wilmette.

Perhaps the most surprising aspect of the current St. Joseph's building is its large size when considering the years of construction. The United States was still suffering through the Great Depression in 1938 and 1939, hence a building of St. Joseph's size, particularly a non-profit church, seems odd. Yet given the extensive finances from Fr. Netstraeter's will and the pressure that the money had to be spent quickly, the excessive height of the church actually makes sense. For the 1940s, few buildings, let alone churches, were as large as St. Joseph's in Chicago's north shore. Although there are dozens of other churches throughout the Chicagoland area that are larger than St. Joseph's — none of them were constructed during the Great Depression.

Concept drawings for the inside of St. Joseph's.

St. Joseph's under construction in 1938 or 1939.

"Put the Money into Brick" 191

The interior of St. Joseph's under construction in 1939.

The north side and roof of St. Joseph's church

The Build Up to War

If the $300,000 had remained in Germany, there's no question that the Nazis would have utilized the money for government purposes. However, Hitler soon had larger objectives than concerning himself with revenge against a Cardinal in America over an public insult.

In 1938, Hitler successfully incorporated his home country of Austria into Germany. This was followed with the Munich Agreement in September, which granted Hitler the Sudetenland (an area of western Czechoslovakia with a heavy German population). That same year, as St. Joseph's new edifice was being constructed, the Nazis closed all of the Catholic schools in Germany, converting them into public facilities (churches were still allowed to remain open).

In the summer of 1939, as the new St. Joseph's church in Wilmette was in its final months of construction, Jews from Germany, Poland, Austria, parts of the Soviet Union, and other conquered countries had been segregated into ghettos: isolated areas of extreme poverty and miserable living conditions. From the ghettos, the Nazis systematically murdered Jews through starvation, random shootings, and deportation to concentration camps.

On September 1, 1939, Germany outraged the majority of Europe by invading Poland and overthrowing the government in a mere three days. On September 3, England and France formally declared war on Germany, marking the official start of World War II.

Cardinal Mundelein Dedicates the new St. Joseph's Church

On September 24, 1939, two weeks after Germany conquered Poland, the new St. Joseph's parish formally opened its doors to the public. Cardinal Mundelein dedicated the new church in a ceremony where he praised the parishioners' unending faith and devotion to their parish and its patron saint. St. Joseph's was the 205th new church building establishment during Cardinal Mundelein's tenure… and his last.

The dedication of St. Joseph's Church in Wilmette was Cardinal Mundelein's last public appearance before his untimely death. On Monday, October 2, 1939, Mundelein suffered an unexpected heart attack and died at the age of 67 in his sleep (obituaries reported that the Cardinal was in "good health"). The Chicago Tribune reported that the city "will have seen its first funeral of a prince of the Catholic church." (2)

The floodgates opened to cement the prolific Cardinal's legacy: sympathetic stories, global accomplishments and impassioned tales highlighting his devout demeanor filled newspapers throughout the nation. Cardinal Mundelein received universal praise, with many highlighting the reopening of St. Mary of the Lake Seminary, the expansion of the St. Vincent DePaul Society and of course the "paper hanger" speech from just two years prior.

The Multiverse of History

Make no mistake – the mystery of Fr. Netstraeter' last will is a footnote in World War II history. There are *hundreds* of prominent figures from the World War II era with thousands upon thousands of compelling stories. Nevertheless, the story of this one priest is a perfect example of the intricate multiverse of history.

***

The funding and construction of St. Joseph's Catholic Church in Wilmette was finished the same month that Hitler sparked World War II by attacking Poland. As the Nazi party had slowly corrupted Germany, the immigrant farmers of Grosse Pointe "upheld" their heritage, as reflected through the lineage of St. Joseph's Parish and the villages across the North Shore. By the 1930s, these offspring of German immigrants had literally built a church — a symbol of hospitality and fellowship, and a school — a symbol of education and growth — out of brick financed by the American capitalist mindset of an immigrant, William Netstraeter. Furthermore, the "German" brick of St. Joseph's church was almost stolen by the Nazis, hence, since 1939, St. Joseph's Catholic Church in Wilmette has always been an indirect rejection of the Nazis' evil ideology.

The funds of this church building were provided by a German immigrant, who is today viewed as a pseudo-godfather of the community at large.

The name of the parish itself, *Saint Joseph*, based off a historical figure famous for the trade of carpentry, implies the physical hands-on job which creates a domestic homestead. It's implied that Joseph *passed down* the carpentry trade to Jesus, the "messiah," whom Fr. Netstraeter devoted his life to through the priesthood. Fr. Netstraeter fulfills the role of a pseudo-carpenter, physically building a new community through his projects and real estate endeavors. Given the age of St. Joseph's in Wilmette, and its "siblings" (St. Henry's in Chicago, St. Peters in Skokie and OLPH in Glenview), a tradition of building and expansion has been *passed down* to future generations.

The connection between Jesus, the "messiah", the promised deliverer of the Jewish people, and Moses remains the foundation of the entire Christian faith. In the story of Moses, Hebrew children were killed off as they were believed to be a threat towards the established power. In the story of Joseph, Mary and Jesus, Jewish children were killed off as they were believed to be a threat to the established power.

"Put the Money into Brick"   197

St. Joseph's Roman Catholic Church in Wilmette: the "gift" Fr. Netstraeter gave to his community.

Unbeknownst to him, the physical building itself would become an unofficial denouncement of Adolf Hitler and the Nazi Party that wreaked havoc throughout his home country of Germany.

THIS CHVRCH ERECTED
TO THE GLORY OF GOD
AND THE HONOR OF
SAINT JOSEPH
IN MEMORY OF REV.
WILLIAM NETSTRAETER
PASTOR OF THIS PARISH
1872 TO 1923

The cornerstone (north-west side) of St. Joseph's Church in Wilmette.

The interior of St. Joseph's from the altar facing the congregation.

By the time we reach modern history, Jewish children were killed off as they were believed to be a threat towards the established power. Although that killing spread to millions of adults as well, not to mention to the killing of German "youths" on the various battlefields of World War II, the same evil dynamic is at work: a deterioration of society and culture.

Hitler himself lamented about the emigration of the German people from their fatherland during World War II, saying:

> Our country today is overpopulated, and the numbers emigrating to America are incredible. How I wish we had the German-Americans with us still! In so far as there are any decent people in America, they are all of German origin.(3)

Considering the likes of Fr. Fortmann, Fr. Netstraeter and Anton Poesch, Hitler's statement is true. However, Hitler would be disappointed to know that the German immigrants didn't see themselves as superior beings or tried to rid the United States of anyone who was different.

Through Fr. Netstraeter's spirit of service, the history of the German immigrants to the United States in the 1800s would grow and spread.

Epilogue:
(1945 to 1956)

Joseph of Nazareth's final mention in the Bible is when Jesus was approximately 12 years old. Joseph is believed to have died before Jesus began his "public ministry" preaching and performing miracles.

Father Johann N. Fortmann oversaw the construction of another 40 x 26 foot frame church in Chicago in 1851. The next year, St. Henry's Church was formally dedicated. Fr. Fortmann remained at St. Henry's until 1866.

Father Bernard Heskemann is believed to have had a nervous breakdown in the wake of St. Joseph's financial nightmare. He went into cloistered life with the Franciscan Friars in Indianapolis, Indiana. He died on July 1, 1894.

Anton Poesch died December 22, 1899, at the age of 88. He is buried in St. Joseph's cemetery.

Mallinckrodt currently serves two functions. The majority of the building is used as condominiums for the retired. The Wilmette Park District operates a section of the building for community use, as well oversees the care of the Mallinckrodt Park.

In the late 1980s **New Tier Township High School** expanded to a second campus 3 miles west of the original campus. Throughout the 1990s, the 2000s and the 2010s, the school was regularly ranked as one of the best high schools in the United States. In the early 2000s, the enrollment exceeded 4,000 students. Alumni from the school have included Charlton Heston, Bob Dole, Bruce Dern, Donald Rumsfeld, Edward Zwick, Rainn Wilson and Liz Phair.

Despite the patriotic passion and economic brilliance of its leaders, the **Nazi Party** was doomed to fail on account of their secular pride. Christians would point out their major flaw for believing in the design of a perfect human specimen without any sort of faith in a divine overseer.

On December 11, 1941, Nazi Germany formally declared war on the United States. One month later, on January 20, 1942, Nazi officials met in Wannsee, a suburb of Berlin to discuss and implement "The Final Solution." The cryptically named plan had one objective: the extermination of the Jewish people. The drama of World War II and its battles raging across Europe and Africa was a perfect distraction for the Nazis' heinous designs. The Final Solution allowed the segregation and murder of Jews on a larger scale and faster than in the late 1930s. Jewish people were quickly shipped off to semi-rural concentration camps where they were exploited for free physical labor, until they were no longer fit to work.

On June 6, 1944, the United States commenced Operation: Overlord (commonly known as D-Day), when the Allied forces invaded northern France by way of beach landings. Throughout the second half of 1944, the Allied forces made their way towards Germany — the United States and Britain from the west and Russia from the east. As the Allied forces sandwiched Nazi Germany, they made terrifying discoveries. In the final year of World War II, the Allied forces slowly began realizing a side of Nazism that seemed unfathomable.

On July 23, 1944, Soviet troops discovered the Majdanek camp outside the Polish city of Lublin, which displayed signs of death on a massive scale. Mass graves, large flaky ashes, various human remains and abandoned clothing all pointed toward the horrific obvious: that tens of thousands of people lost their lives at this work camp. There were a few hundred survivors, many suffering from illness, who detailed their living conditions and the Nazis' methods to the Soviets.

Majdanek was discovered early in the Allied forces' push towards Berlin. The vast majority of Jews here were killed through gas chambers and shootings. Those seen unfit for labor (children, the elderly, the disabled) were killed immediately and not even registered as inmates of a camp.

Five months later, on January 16, 1945, Hitler went into refuge in a bunker within the capital of Berlin with his closest officers and advisors.

Over a week later, on January 27, the Soviets would find another concentration camp by the name of Auschwitz. The deadliest of all the camps, it is estimated that 1.1 million Jews were murdered at Auschwitz throughout the timespan of the war. Catholic figures, Saint Edith Stein and Saint Maximilian Kolbe, were also murdered at Auschwitz.

In the month of April 1945 alone, another *seven* camps were discovered and liberated; *three* more camp discoveries followed in May.

On May 7, 1945, Nazi Germany unconditionally surrendered to the Allied forces. By this time, over 2,500 Catholics perished at the hands of the Nazis, the majority of them clergy. Additionally, over 6,000,000 Jews were killed.

Epilogue 205

A billboard highlighting Saint Maximilian Kolbe at the Auschwitz Memorial.

Adolf Hitler died on April 30, 1945, ten days after his fifty-sixth birthday. In the bunker, Hitler learned that there was no escape from the invading Russian Soviets. He and his wife, Eva Braun (whom he married the day before), retreated into his private study. Rather than surrender, Adolf Hitler committed suicide in his bunker. He shot himself in the head while Eva bit down on a cyanide capsule. Their bodies were efficiently but ceremoniously carried out of the bunker and set ablaze among the rubble of Berlin.

Joseph Goebbels and his wife, Magda, were also in the bunker during Hitler's last days. The day after Hitler committed suicide, Joseph and Magda murdered their six children, poisoning them with cyanide in their sleep, and then shot each other.

Chicago's **North Shore** has connections to hundreds of veterans who fought evil in World War II. Yet the land on which these suburbs sit were settled by German Christians who believed they were starting a brand new home for future generations.

The German immigrants, particularly those who found and cultivated a homestead in **Skokie**, had no idea of the coming events in the next century and how that very territory would become a sanctuary for post-World War II Jews.

After World War II, the Jewish population of Chicago grew rapidly, with their culture and faith thriving. The early 1950s saw synagogues and congregations form in the Village of Skokie, close to the pre-established congregation in the Rogers Park neighborhood. After the establishing of these synagogues, the number of Jewish families increased steadily, thanks in part to the cheaper land, affordable housing and opening of the Edens Expressway in 1951. Approximately a half-century later in 1995, historian Peter d'A. Jones noted that:

> [The] northern suburbs of Niles, Evanston, Wilmette, Glenview, Winnetka, Morton Grove, and Northbrook is believed to be 10

to 25 percent Jewish... Glencoe, Highland Park, Skokie, and Lincolnwood [are] estimated as close to 50 percent Jewish.

The immigration of Jews into Chicago and its suburbs is not inherently due to the German Christians. However, the contrast between Nazi Germany, seeking to exile Jews, and Chicago's northern "German" territory welcoming Jews is a stark contrast. Additionally, the formation of **Memorial Park Cemetery** benefitted these Jewish families as they made use of it throughout the second half of the 1900s. Today, Memorial Park is primarily a Jewish cemetery.

The Holocaust Monument in the Village Green Park in downtown Skokie.

Cardinal George Mundelein was buried behind the main altar of the chapel at St. Mary of the Lake Seminary. Although not officially, the seminary has become known as "Mundelein Seminary" throughout the Midwest.

Mundelein's personal architect, **Joseph McCarthy**, is credited with fifteen church designs under his own name and an additional ten under his firm's name, *McCarthy, Smith and Eppig* — all throughout Illinois, but mostly the Chicagoland area. McCarthy died in Oak Park, Illinois in July 1965 at the age of 81.

Upon the completion of a large brand new school building, **Father John Neumann** and St. Joseph's Parish received a letter of congratulations from President Franklin D. Roosevelt. During the teardown of the old church and the construction of the new, Mass was celebrated in the new school's gymnasium. In April 1939, in the wake of the legal dispute, Fr. Neumann was elevated to the title of Very Reverend Monsignor. In 1952, Monsignor Neumann orchestrated a new convent for the School Sisters of St. Francis, about a half mile west of St. Joseph's, on the land that Fr. Netstraeter had owned, next to the Mallinckrodt property. Monsignor Neumann's final construction project was completed in 1959 when part of the school was annexed to the church.

Monsignor Neumann remained pastor of St. Joseph's until his death on January 23, 1964.

Due to the age of **St. Joseph's Catholic Church**, it has been honored with a variety of acknowledgements throughout the years, being the second oldest parish in the Archdiocese of Chicago, surviving three economic crises (1873, 1929, 2008), having the oldest Women's Club in the Archdiocese and closing and reopening the school in the timespan of twelve years (1986 to 1998). The parish was formally renamed "Historic St. Joseph's Church" in the late-2000s. In 2016, the parish received the Sesquicentennial Award by the Illinois State Historic Society.

St. Joseph's would acquire an unofficial nickname in the 2000s when Rev. Jerome Listecki (a weekend assistant) and Rev. Francis Kane (pastor) were named Bishops in 2001 and 2003 respectively. The term "cathedral" is reserved for a church where a bishop resides. Given the gothic aesthetic of St. Joseph's church compared to the other Catholic churches in Chicago's north shore, it caused the parish secretary, Maria Friedrich, to quip that St. Joseph's was the "Cathedral of the North Shore." After Maria's death in December 2008, the phrase took on a life of its own and was attributed to her as a memoriam, as she dedicated so much of her life to the parish.

The *only* plausible way **Fr. William Netstraeter** would have even heard the name "Adolf Hitler" during his lifetime would have been in his final months alive when the events of the Munich Beer Hall Putsch and the subsequent trial were headlines in Germany. Hitler was sentenced to prison on April 1, 1924. Fr. Netstraeter died April 7. Some presumed that Hitler's incarceration was the end of his political career.

Although Fr. Netstraeter died before Hitler's rise to power, his dedication to St. Joseph's community was the opposite of Nazi ideology, which was soon to terrorize his home country. Where Fr. Netstraeter acquired land for fellowship, Hitler would demand land for power.

The idea that Fr. Netstraeter parallels Joseph of Nazareth reaches the core of general Christian teaching: to be "Christ-like." While the Nazis preached individuality as an avenue to *escape* religion (and ultimately conform to *their* ideology), Fr. Netstraeter attempted to *bring* people together.

Fr. Netstraeter's vision of a German American community in 1945 brought forth a thriving school, including 500 registered families in St. Joseph's Parish.

For years following, Germany would face global embarrassment and scorn for the Holocaust as the death toll tallied into the millions; Nazi leadership spurred the darkest days for Germany. By 1956, St. Joseph's would more than double in size.

Fr. Netstraeter was not merely a good pastor who grew his community according to the German Catholic traditions. His land acquisitions display a spirit of service; he built a community, not just a source of personal financial income for himself. Throughout his life, the money went back to his Catholic homestead in the various construction projects, including his prominent posthumous church.

Fr. Netstraeter's grave in St. Joseph's cemetery, with his posthumous church on the other side of the street.

Acknowledgements

There are three people(s) that we were the spark for making this book come to fruition: Nancy Canafax, Monsignor John Pollard and the Henik family. All had a significant role in shaping *Cathedral of the North Shore* in 2012 & 2013, and they were key components all these years later in telling the full biography.

This process began in September 2009 with Monsignor Pollard's enthusiasm for Fr. Netstraeter's forgotten story. The first formal "research" of the history done in 2012 for the documentary was helped along by Monsignor Pollard sharing his insight of the history. Taking on a more meticulous study in 2019 was equally encouraged by St. Joseph's beloved former pastor.

In early 2012, thanks to John Henik, *Cathedral of the North Shore* went into production and released the following year. It was the first time that Fr. Netstraeter's story was given widespread attention – not merely in a cinematic format, but with the media attention that followed in the wake of the film. This never would have happened without John agreeing to use the history for his video evangelization project. His wife, Anette, and daughter, Jennifer, were supportive and helpful throughout the year-long filmmaking process. In the subsequent years the Henik's remained dear friends to both us and our family. When we told them that we were going to do this book, they were exceptionally helpful, Jennifer particularly, in getting us access to incredible historical materials that really brought this book to life.

Finally — Super Bowl Sunday 2019, in the middle of the (frankly, dull) game — Nancy Canafax sent Michael an e-mail with an image of the bronze plaque of New Trier High School's founding members. Although the plaque wasn't unveiled until late April, it marked the first time that Fr. Netstraeter was going to be formally recognized by local government. Nancy's dedication in keeping the history alive of St. Joseph's Parish and Fr. Netstraeter alive was what truly the seed of the "literary adaptation" idea. From the moment we decided to tackle this project in mid-March, Nancy Canafax was who we (playfully "blamed") for inspiring us to write this book. More importantly, Nancy was whom we wanted to make the most proud of — not in that we wrote some masterpiece — rather that she could see her work inspire us to take the next steps in preserving this story.

***

Although we've grown apart from the St. Joseph's family over the years, as we embarked on this task… to say that "supportive words" from Mary Pat Buckley, Mary Lou DiClementi and Kirsten Solmos were "very much appreciated" is an understatement. All three graciously give us time in conversations that were more help than they probably realized. Our moral

Acknowledgements 215

stamina in writing *Rev. William Netstraeter* was in credit to them.

We want to pay credit to Dr. Laurence F. Knapp, who taught both of us in college in a variety of film courses. Although the material from those classes didn't apply for this book, Dr. Knapp's emphasis on research, particularly for an academic undertaking like this, was totally an influence in this project.

A special thanks to Debbi Brotz and Shelly Taylor of St. Francis de Sales Seminary in Wisconsin for cross-referencing our dates *and* even providing us with the notations from the 1860s register!

As we went through the text tying up historical loose ends, Meg Romero Hall, Director of Archives and Records Center at the Archdiocese of Chicago, was very helpful in answering our random questions.

Upon finding some of Fr. Netstraeter's actual hundred-year-old titles and deeds in the archives, we are very grateful to Natasha Zikova for going through them and explaining them to us from a real estate perspective.

In 2012, the great Patrick Leary of the Wilmette Historical Museum was incredibly generous with his time in helping Michael learn about Fr. Netstraeter. In 2019, particularly with the history of the Gross Point taverns, Mr. Leary was an outstanding teacher and really helped us flush out our perspective of Fr. Netstraeter. We are lucky if our book is a mere fraction of how interesting it is listening to Mr. Leary talk about North Shore history.

A big shout-out to Tita Camilotes at St. Henry's Parish in Chicago who helped shine some light on the whereabouts of Fr. J. Fortmann after he disappeared from our research.

Fr. Netstraeter's cause of death was a bit of a mystery that we were luckily able to uncover! We owe a giant word of thanks to Larry Biela, Kelly Venticinque and her father, Paul Venticinque, for walking us through the steps of obtaining Fr. Netstraeter's death certificate.

Thank you Terry Luc at Our Lady of Perpetual Help in Glenview for uncovering one of the old photographs of OLPH for us to reprint.

The managers of the Wilmette Park District of the Mallinckrodt Community Center, Julie Mantice & Penny Bashford, were super kind and helpful in pointing us in the direction of material. In fact, it was because of them...

We were able to connect with Sister Maryann Warwick and Sister Anastasia Sanford who helped us acquire a wonderful old image of the Mallinckrodt property from the Sisters of Christian Charity.

In the final stages, Nancy Wagner at the Wilmette Public Library was terrific in helping us tie up loose ends.

Then of course came the superheroes: Jonas Dargis, Amanda Lindsey and Brian Solmos who were given premature manuscripts of this book and returned with some of the best feedback for fine-tuning the flow of the narrative.

Of this "test team", the great Gerry Munley (and history of New Trier expert) gave the book a detailed overlook and really helped sharpen a number of the minute details.

Of course, our family and friends are a key element in our lives. Our accomplishments are in credit to them: Mike & Carleen Jolls, Tim Jolls, Jennifer Jolls, George Mohrlein, Rita Murphy, Robert Murphy, Jim & Sue Murphy, Bob & Jen Murphy and their kids, Hunter, Brianna and Connor, Jim Murphy, Katie Murphy, John Murphy, Mary & Jose Quintero, Katie Quintero, Matt Quintero, Rev. Richard Simon and Rev. William Welsh.

Finally - of course, our endless gratitude to Fr. Netstraeter himself for living a life that still inspires us to this day.

Daniel Jolls would like to thank:

I *suppose* it's only appropriate to thank my brother first for asking me to co-write this book. Without his dedication and passion for Fr. Netstraeter, I would have seen this fascinating story as nothing more than interesting footnote of Chicagoland history. Instead, it's given me insight on why *individual* parish history and vitality is so important, and clarity in why we as Catholics gravitate towards sacred, traditional ceremonials.

To Mr. Tom Herman – you started out as my 7th grade English teacher and became one of my closest, lifelong friends. You know me better than I know myself. You were my Confirmation sponsor (at St. Joseph's, no less) and have continued to be the strongest positive influence in my life. Thank you for teaching me how to write, how to care about writing, and most importantly, how to enjoy it. Hopefully this is the start of a path to us writing a book together some day.

To the St. John Paul II Newman Center of UIC – I wouldn't have graduated college if it wasn't for this wonderful place. When I started at UIC in the fall of 2015, I just wanted a place to maybe go to Mass once a week. By my graduation, I was the president of the Newman Catholic Student Organization because everyone there strived to welcome me. As changes rock the Archdiocese of Chicago, I can only hope and pray that the Newman Center continues to be an inspiring and unique environment for UIC students. Fr. Patrick Marshall, thank you for being my closest confidant and mentor for three years. You gave me the confidence to move forward in all my endeavors. Sister Diane Collins, thank you for your tireless efforts to make the Newman Center a thriving house of God, all while making it look so easy. Becca Siar, thank you for teaching me how to handle the pressures of a leadership role and for continuing to be a loyal and supportive friend.

To Jake Raffe – thanks for hanging out until the wee hours of the morning multiple times in the process of writing this book, letting me vent about…well, everything. Your dedication as a loving husband and father inspires me to no end. And therefore, thank you Heather Raffe for letting your husband stay out so late.

To Yongjin Yi – my fellow English major partner-in-crime, thank you for keeping things light and encouraging me to move forward, no matter how frustrated I was. Your perspectives on philosophy, history, literature, and pretty much anything else will always fascinate me and keep me yearning for discussion.

To Abi Whitten – I can't thank you enough for the prayers, the positive reinforcement, the prayers, the happy-go-lucky attitude, the dinners, the prayers, the multiple three-hour-long phone calls, the prayers…did I mention the prayers? You were one of the first to know about this book, and were eager to help in any way since day one. Holy Thursday 2019 in particular was unforgettable as I eagerly showed you sample covers as we went church-hopping. Thank you for your input, love and support.

To my college advisors and professors – you went above and beyond in your efforts to teach your respective classes and help us students contribute to the hectic college environment. Specifically, I would like to thank Dr. Sara Hall, Dr. Margena Christian, Dr. Laura

Dingeldein, Marsha Cassidy, Ralph Cintron, Helen Ward Page, and Alfred Thomas.

To my friends past & present – I'm blessed to have so many wonderful people in my life who inspire me in different ways – so many people that I humbly ask you not be offended if I forget you. You all influence me in ways you can't possibly fathom: Emily Blatter, Edwin & Luis Castaneda, Tito Fernandez, Fr. John Grieco, Dan Gurber, Samantha Hernandez, Vianka Herrera, Nathan Hurde, Tom Kelly, Ben Kuruvilla, Patrick Lechner, Jeremy Mazur, Fr. Timothy Monahan, Aida Pabello, Fr. Carlos Paniagua-Monroy, Mark Perkowski, Michelle Pullorkunnel, Daryl Ranario, Jonathan Rivera, Kasia Soprych, Roshin Varghese, Tom Weidner, Meri Whitten and Josh Ytem.

Michael Jolls would like to thank:

In 2012, I had three incredible friends that were willing to go along with *Cathedral of the North Shore*. To this day, Clint Cottrell, Natalia Samoylova and Bobby Watson have remained three of the most instrumental collaborators I work with, and each made a significant artistic contribution to this book — particularly Clint who thankfully still had a digital copy of the images.

The staff of Queen of All Saints who put up with my idiosyncrasies: Rev. Simon Braganza, Bobby Brooks, Cathy Carroll, Rev. Walter Cheboi, Steven

Chorak, John Conway, Mary Cronin, Rev. Michael Cronin, Moira Dargis, Shannon Divane, Kate Dombrowski, Janet Dugan, Jerry Farrell, Rev. Edward Grace, Pam Hautzinger, Kellie Halkitis, Sara Hermez, Jonathon Hernandez, Dorothy Kennedy, Eric Martinez, Ralph Meschewski, Victor Miranda, Mary Morley, Morgan O'Leary, Amy Jo Parker, Monsignor John Pollard, Paul Scavone, Donna Simons, Ken Skokowski, Erika Tate and Rev. Michael Trail.

On that note, I'd like to highlight Dr. Carole Eipers, whose experience in publishing as vice president of Sadlier publishing has always been tremendously helpful with my endless questions. I'd also like to thank Dr. Ken Sotak who has taught me countless grammatical points, dozens of stylistic tips and much appreciated words of encouragement.

Now... who else...? I think I should personally give a big fat special thanks to the crack team that decided, PURELY for making a political statement, to dissolve two healthy parishes against their wills. As a former grade school student of *both* St. Francis Xavier's (1995 to 1998) *and* St. Joseph's (1998 to 2000), the mandated merge while we were writing this book became a good reason to preserve this history... but I won't go down the rabbit hole on this point.

To my friends – your mere existence means more to me and was helpful in ways you aren't aware: Nick Allexon, Tina Boivin, Kadri Cevrem, Eric S.

Cunningham, Sara Gorman, Alexa Hartfield, Kristine Homan, Mike Wade Johnson of *Faux Pas Films*, Jessica Kearney, James Kim, Olia Klein, Liza Kudas, Anastasia Lincoln, Karol Matejko, Cleveland Moore, Anna Nadolskaya, Siobhán Regan, Alla Royfman, Don Shanahan, Jennifer Sparks, Stacy White and Denise Gavlak Yemc.

List of Photographs

12 --- St. Joseph's Roman Catholic Church bulletin cover of September 13, 2009. Public image.

38 --- "Flight into Egypt," oil painting by Eugène Girardet. PD – US – expired.

41 --- The Schmidt-Behrmann Log House, located in Winnetka, Illinois. Photo by Michael Jolls.

44 --- "A Bit of Nature Near Wilmette, IL." From the St. Joseph Parish archives; acquired 2012.

47 --- Chart of prices, taken from Herbert B. Mulford's *Frontiers of Old Wilmette*. Published through the Wilmette Life of 1952 and 1953. Chart created by Michael Jolls.

48 --- Gross Point farmer with cow. From the St. Joseph Parish archives; acquired 2012.

48 --- Gross Point farmers with tractors. From the St. Joseph Parish archives; acquired 2012.

49 --- Gross Point farmers with tractor tilling field. From the St. Joseph Parish archives; acquired 2012.

49 --- Gross Point farm with three women. From the St. Joseph Parish archives; acquired 2012.

50 --- Gross Point farms. From the St. Joseph Parish archives; acquired 2012.

50 --- Children on a Gross Point farm. From the St. Joseph Parish archives; acquired 2012.

51 --- Women with cow in Gross Point. From the St. Joseph Parish archives; acquired 2012.

51 --- Women working the field in Gross Point. From the St. Joseph Parish archives; acquired 2012.

54 --- Sign outside of St. Joseph's Catholic Church depicting the log cabin. Photo by Michael Jolls.

55 --- Concept art by Mary Delany. From the St. Joseph's Parish archives; acquired 2012.

69 --- Image depicting Ridge Road, facing north. Description reads, "Ridge Rd. North of Shiller. Gross Point ILL". From the St. Joseph's Parish archives; acquired 2012.

80 --- Photograph of the oldest sacramental book in St. Joseph's records. Photograph and editing by Michael Jolls.

82 --- Bishop Thomas P. Foley photographed circa 1870. Public Domain as of January 1, 1924.

89 --- 1869 map of Chicago, highlighting the area destroyed by the fire. Public Domain as of January 1, 1924.

92 --- Anton Poesch. From the St. Joseph's Parish archives; acquired 2012.

98 --- St. Joseph School class of 1890. From the St. Joseph's Parish archives; acquired 2012.

99 --- St. Joseph School. From the St. Joseph's Parish archives; acquired 2012.

99 --- Classroom inside of St. Joseph School. From the St. Joseph's Parish archives; acquired 2012.

100 --- St. Joseph's Church photographed in circa 1870. From the St. Joseph's Parish archives; acquired 2012. St. Peter's Catholic Church in Skokie. Photography and editing by Michael Jolls.

100 --- Scan of cover of St. Joseph Parish report. From the St. Joseph's Parish archives; acquired 2012.

101 --- View of St. Joseph's Cemetery. Image from the Wilmette Historical Museum. Reprinted with permission.

101 --- Interior of the old St. Joseph's Church. From the St. Joseph's Parish archives; acquired 2012.

103 --- Franz Netstraeter memorial photo. June 1907. From the St. Joseph's Parish archives; acquired 2012.

107 --- Elm Forest of the North. Image from the Wilmette Historical Museum. Reprinted with permission.

114 --- Wilmette motherhouse circa 1920, areal view. Permission for reprinted from Sisters of Christian Charity – Western Region Archives.

Lists of Photographs   225

115 --- The old church of Our Lady of Perpetual Help, believed to be taken in March 1925. Image from Our Lady of Perpetual help. Reprinted with permission.

116 --- Entrance of Memorial Park Cemetery; Skokie Boulevard entrance. Photography by Michael Jolls.

122 --- Father William Netstraeter. From the St. Joseph's Parish archives; acquired 2012.

128 --- First New Trier High School Student Body, 1901. Faculty and students pose in front of newly-completed building after high school opened for classes in February, 1901. Found in *Wilmette: A History* by George D. Bushnell. Wilmette Bicentennial Commission. Village of Wilmette. 1976. 1997. Page 113 (both editions). Reprinted with permission of New Trier Township High School.

133 --- Three gentlemen in a Gross Point bar. From the St. Joseph's Parish archives; acquired 2012.

134 --- John Mick's tavern. From the St. Joseph's Parish archives; acquired 2012.

142 --- Cardinal George Mundelein. Public Domain. Copyright term of plus 70 years.

148 --- Father William Netstraeter outside of the rectory. From the St. Joseph's Parish archives; acquired 2012.

151 --- Image of Father William Netstraeter's Last Will & Testament. Screenshot from *Cathedral of the North Shore* (2013).

157 --- *Vienna State Opera House* by Adolf Hitler. 1912. Public Domain. Copyright term of plus 70 years.

158 --- *Outskirts of a town with bridge and figures* by Adolf Hitler. 1909. Public Domain. Copyright term of plus 70 years.

158 --- *The Courtyard of the Old Residency in Munich* by Adolf Hitler. 1914. Public Domain. Copyright term of plus 70 years.

159 --- *Mother Mary with the Holy Child Jesus* by Adolf Hitler. 1913. Public Domain. Copyright term of plus 70 years.

159 --- *House to a lake with mountains* by Adolf Hitler. 1910. Public Domain. Copyright term of plus 70 years.

162 --- Adolf Hitler in the early 1920s. Photographed believed to have been taken between 1920 to 1924. Public Domain. Copyright term of plus 70 years.

165 --- Auszeichnung des Hitlerjungen Willi Hübner. Photographer unknown. Bundesarchiv, Bild 183-J31305/CC-BY-SA 3.0.

169 --- Berlin, Pressempfang mit Goebbels und Hitler. Bundesarchiv, Bild 102-14492/CC-BY-SA 3.0.

178 --- Franklin D. Roosevelt and Cardinal Mundelein in Albany, New York. November 18, 1932. National Archives and Records Administrations cooperation project. Public Domain.

190 --- Sketch drawings of St. Joseph's Church, dated 1939. St. Joseph's Parish archives.

190 --- St. Joseph Church under construction in 1938 or 1939. St. Joseph's Parish archives; acquired 2012.

191 --- St. Joseph Church inside of construction. 1939. St. Joseph's Parish archives; acquired 2012.

197 --- Front of St. Joseph's Catholic Church. Image from St. Joseph's Catholic Church. Reprinted with permission.

198 --- Cornerstone of St. Joseph's Church. Photography by Mark Dunn.

192 --- St. Joseph's Church rooftop taken from the bell tower in 2012. Photography by Michael Jolls.

198 --- Sanctuary of St. Joseph's Church. Screenshot from *Cathedral of the North Shore* (2013).

198 --- Billboard testimonial to St. Maximillian Kolbe in Auschwitz. September 2016. Photography by Dennis Jarvis.

200 --- Holocaust Monument in Village Green Park. Skokie, Illinois. Photography by Michael Jolls.

203 --- St. Joseph's Cemetery. Photography by Michael Jolls.

203 --- Gravestone of Father William Netstraeter. Photography by Michael Jolls.

Endnotes

Chapter One – St. Joseph and the Flight to Egypt
1. The Gospel of Matthew. Chapter 2, verse 13. *The New American Bible*. St. Benedict Press. 2011.
2. The Catholic Church believes that these children, murdered by King Herod, are the first Christian martyrs. The Feast of the Holy Innocents is traditionally celebrated/remembered on December 28 in the Catholic faith.
3. Ibid. (1)
4. Ibid. (1)

Chapter Two – The German Immigrants
1. The name of "Grosse Pointe" came from the French explorers in the late 1690s.
2. Reverend F.L. Kalvelage, *The Survey of Saint Joseph Parish*. September 1930. Hubbard Woods, Illinois.
3. Herbert B. Mulford, *Frontiers of Old Wilmette*. The Wilmette Life; reprinting. 1952 & 1953. Published in 1954.
4. Ibid. (2)
5. Ibid. (2)
6. According to Fr. Kalvelage's history this was Rev. Ostlangenburg. Ibid. (2)

Chapter Three – The Succession of Pastors
1. Author Unknown. "St. Joseph's Church First to Observe Centennial." The Wilmette Life. 1947.
2. Reflections on Fr. Fortmann; the following came from Right Reverend Bishop Vandevelde's diary entry of April 21st, 1850 which says:
"Third Sunday of Easter. Said Mass at eight o'clock at Gross Point Church; forty persons made their first communion of whom three were converts. At ten o'clock blessed the new frame church (70 x 30). Dedicated in honor of St. Joseph. High Mass by the Rev. J. N. Fortmann, the pastor, at which I assisted with cope and mitre, together with Rev. Father Di Maria and Rev. M. Hampston, sub-deacon and Mr. Laymacher in dalmatics. After Mass exhortation on Confirmation in German,

confirmed forty-nine males and thirty-two females. Assisted at Vespers. Heavy thunderstorms at night."
Reverend F.L. Kalvelage, *The Survey of Saint Joseph Parish*. September 1939. Hubbard Woods, Illinois.
3. An excerpt from one of the "Hoffman Letters". The text appears in all of St. Joseph's history albums: 1939. 1980. 1995. 2010.
4. The village of Wilmette didn't incorporate until August 1872, almost a decade after the end of the Civil War. At that time, Wilmette only had approximately 300 residents, so it was fairly detached from the events of the Civil War taking place eastward and southward. Even considering the date that people began coming and inhabiting the Grosse Point area, there is very little Civil War history or references in the Villages of Wilmette, Glenview, Skokie or Evanston. Some have suggested that there are veterans of the Civil War buried in St. Joseph's parish cemetery in Wilmette, although this has never been confirmed.
5. On the formation of St. Peter's in Skokie:
Additionally, St. Mary's in Evanston was founded in 1865, just four miles south of St. Joseph's in Wilmette. The fact that Catholics founded *another* church (St. Peter's) during St. Joseph's most tumultuous years is further evidence of the German Catholics seeing the writing on the wall for St. Joseph's.
6. Ibid. (2)

Chapter Four – A Bargain

1. The annals of St. Francis de Sales Seminary, written in Latin, indicates the following:
Mart 23, Advenit Rev. D. Guilielmus Nettstraeter, subiaconus ex diocese Paderbornersi. (March 23, We admitted Rev. D. William Nettstraeter, a subdeacon from the diocese of Paderborn).
Julii 16, In Ecclesia Cathedrali Milw, ad saurum diaconatus ordinen evecti sunt... Guil Nettstraeter pro dioc. Chicago, ensi (July 16, at the Cathedral of Milwaukee, we ordained to the diaconate William Nettstraeter of the Diocese of Chicago).
Sept 30, Rev, episcopo sacerdotes ordinate sumit Ecclesia Seminari... Guil Nettrater, Chicago (Sept 30, The Rev.

Bishop ordained William Nettrater of Chicago in the Seminary's chapel).
These entries were provided by the office of Achieves & Records Management office at St. Francis de Sales Seminary in St. Francis, Wisconsin. Translations by Shelly Taylor and Daniel Jolls.
2. Mark Dunn, "Monography: Father William Netstraeter."

Chapter Five – Renovation

1. The churches in downtown Chicago that were destroyed in the Great Chicago Fire were Saint Mary's and Church of the Holy Name.
2. The death toll of the Great Chicago Fire is an estimate. Only 150 bodies were recovered.
3. Another source says 100,000 homeless, making it 33.3% of the city's population.
Janet B. Pascal. *What Was the Great Chicago Fire*. Grosset & Dunlap. 2016.
4. Reverend F.L. Kalvelage, *The Survey of Saint Joseph Parish*. September 1930. Hubbard Woods, Illinois.
5. The subject of Fr. Netstraeter completion of the old church remains a mere sentence in four of the parish history articles about him. They read as follows:
"Fr. Netstraeter completed the building program inaugurated by his predecessor." – 1939.
"Next, Father Netstreaeter completed the building program left behind by Father Heskemann." – 1980.
"First he [Netstraeter] *repaired the faults of the newly built church."* – 1995.
"Father Netstraeter gave his immediate attention to the completion of the building project begun by his predecessor." – 2010.
6. Ron Chernow, *Grant*. Penguin Press. 2017.
7. "In 1852 the Frist Plenary Council stated that 'Bishops are exhorted to have a Catholic school in every parish and the teachers should be paid from the parochial funds,' In 1866 the Second Plenary Council stated that 'teachers belonging to religious congregations should be employed when possible in our schools. The latter should be erected in every parish.'"
Mark Dunn, "Monography: Father William Netstraeter."

8. From Mark Dunn's history: "An account by the sisters states that the original wood frame first floor was lifted up and placed on top of a brick structure to create a two-story building."
   Ibid. (7)
9. The Archdiocese of Chicago Archives & Records office shows not mention of Fr. Netstraeter serving on the board of *The New World*. However, Bishop Feehan founded the paper in 1892 and died ten years later. This *suggests* that if Fr. Netstraeter *was* assigned, it would have been between 1892 to 1902 – in the newspaper's early years. Additionally, there is no formal record of *The New World* having financial problems – this is only mentioned in the 1939 history of St. Joseph's by Fr. Kalvelage. The majority of the records about the administration of the Chicago Diocese begins in 1915 with the Cardinal Mundelein era.
10. *Album of Genealogy and Biography, Cook County, Illinois*. Brookhaven Press. 1895.

Chapter Six – Boomtown

1. Mark Dunn, "Monography: Father William Netstraeter".
2. According to Mark Dunn: "From 1844 until 1892, members of the Lauermann family owned the land that is now Mallinckrodt in the Park." The cold water treatment that Mother Alexia underwent in Bacarai was popularized by a priest named Father Sebastian Kneipp.
   Ibid. (1)
3. Ibid. (1)
4. Bob Smith.

Chapter Seven – The Politician

1. George D. Bushnell. *Wilmette: A History*. The Wilmette Bicentennial Commission. Wilmette, Illinois. 1976.
2. Ibid. (1)
3. "Townships", like the one used for New Trier Township High School was government property used for legal parcels of land. From the book *Looking Back*: "Under the [Thomas] Jeffersonian township system, surveyors could work from north-south, and east-west lines of townships, which were each 36 square miles (six miles by six miles). Each township is divided into one mile square."

David C. Leach, Jr. *Looking Back*. Wilmette Historical Museum. 2014.

Chapter Eight – Dry vs. West

1. In August 1917, the United States Senate passed a resolution calling for an amendment to the constitution of the United States, banning the sale and manufacturing of alcohol. In December, that resolution was approved by the House of Representatives. Before the law could go into effect, it needed to be ratified by three-fourths (75%) of the states, which it did throughout the year of 1918. The law finally went into effect on January 20, 1920.
2. John Jacoby. "The North Shore battles against saloons." *The Wilmette Beacon*. October 15, 2015.
3. Reverend F.L. Kalvelage, The Survey of Saint Joseph Parish. September 1930. Hubbard Woods, Illinois.

Chapter Nine – An Era Ends & Another Begins

1. George William Mundelein, *Two Crowded Years; Being Selected Addresses, Pastorals."* First edition published 1923. Reprinted by BibloLife. Also public domain work.
2. At any point in the two-thousand year history of the Roman Catholic Church has there been a maximum 130 Cardinals at the same time during Mundelein's era, there were closer to about 80.
3. Author not specified, "Rev. William Netstraeter of St. Joseph's Parish dies at age of 83, pioneer churchman, was pastor of St. Joseph's for 54 years." *The Wilmette Life*. April 11, 1924.

Chapter Ten – The Rise of National Socialism in Germany

1. From the book, *Hitler: Ascent 1889-1939*: "112 candidates applied. Hitler survived the first round of tests in which 33 people were rejected. In the second round, of the remaining, only 28 applicants were accepted by the school. In *Mein Kampf* he called the failure, "an abrupt blow from nowhere." When Hitler inquired why he failed, the academy director told him that his talent lay in architecture, not art." Volker Ullrich, *Hitler: Ascent 1889-1939*. Knopf, Borzoi Books. Translated by Jefferson Chase. 2016.

2. Ibid. (1)
3. Hitler's father, Alois, died in 1903, but Hitler was only 13 at the time, making him too young to receive money from Alois' estate. Once Hitler turned 22 could he receive the inheritance.
   Ibid. (1)
4. Adolf Hitler, *Mein Kampf*, as translated from Jefferson Chase.
   Ibid. (1)
5. The change in name was for popularity's sake, as people would be more apt to joining a party of National Socialism over any sort of Communist affiliation, as Communists were blamed for defeating Germany in World War I.
6. Ibid. (1)
7. A.N. Wilson, *Hitler*, Basic Books. March 2012.
8. Ibid. (7)
9. Hitler's presence was so important to the Nazis that a mutiny rose because some wanted to merge with a rival political party, the German Socialist Party and Hitler planned to resign.
10. Dr. Michael Sullivan, *An Eroding Milieu? Catholic Youth, Church Authority, and Popular Behavior in Northwest Germany During the Third Reich, 1933-1938.* Marist College. 2004.
11. Ibid. (10)
12. Anthony Read. *The Devil's Disciples: Hitler's Inner Circle.* W.W. Norton & Company Inc. 2003.
13. Ibid (12)

Chapter Eleven – A Battle of Words

1. John Cornwell. *Hitler's Pope: The Secret History of Pius XII.* Viking Press. Published by the Penguin Group. 1999.
2. "Representations Follow Prelate's Attack on Hitler." *The Evening Star*. Washington D.C. 20 May 1937. Page 1. Library of Congress.
3. David King, *The Trial of Adolf Hitler: The Beer Hallf Putsch and the Rise of Nazi Germany*. W.W. Norton & Company Inc. 2017.
4. The popularity of the "Austrian Paperhanger" nick-name has stuck. In Mel Brooks' 2001 musical remake of *The Producers*, the flamboyant Adolf, during the faux

production of "Springtime for Hitler" says: *"I was just a paperhanger, no one more obscurer."*
5. John Jacoby. "Father William Netstraeter 2." Wilmette Beacon. Wilmette. 11 May 2011.
6. Ibid. (5)

Chapter Twelve – "Put the Money Into Brick"
1. Edward R. Kantowicz. *Corporation Sole*. University of Notre Dame Press. 1983.
2. Rev. John Evans. "Plan Majestic Funeral Rittes for Cardinal Mundelein." *Chicago Daily Tribune*. Chicago. 3 October 1939. Page 1. ProQuest Historical Newspapers.
3. A.N. Wilson. *Hitler*. Basic Books. March 2012.

Epilogue
1. Peter d'A. Jones. *Ethnic Chicago: A Multicultural Portrait*. William B. Eerdmans Publishing Company. 1995

Index

Does not include the Endnotes.
Only references the primary text.

18th Amendment, 138

Academy of Fine Arts, Vienna, 155, 156
Africa (country),
Alexia, Mother, 108, 109, 110, 112, 113
Allied Forces, 29, 30, 203, 204
Annexation Club, The, 123, 124
Anti-Saloon League, 130, 131, 137
Apple, 133
Archdiocese of Chicago, 15, 17, 28, 52, 61, 64, 126, 141, 142, 182, 183, 184, 186, 209
Auschwitz, 204

Babylonia (country), 34
Baha'i Temple, 190
Bavaria (region), 27, 109, 161
Beer Hall Putsch (see "Munich Beer Hall Putsch")
Benedict XVI, Pope, 11
Berlin (city), 146, 202, 204, 205
Bethlehem (city), 34, 35, 37
Braun, Eva, 205
Britain (country), 28, 203
Brothers of Charity, 171
Bushnell, George B., 79, 123

Canafax, Nancy, 14
Cathedral of the North Shore (film), 13, 14
Cathedral of the North Shore (title), 209, 210
Canada (country), 40
Chernow, Ron, 39
Chicago Tribune, 108, 194
Cologne Cathedral, 168
Cook County, 54, 110, 183
Czechoslovakia, 193

David (Biblical King), 37
D-Day, 203
Declaration of Independence,
Dern, Bruce,
Diocese of Chicago — see "Archdiocese of Chicago"
Disney (company), 133
Disney, Walt, 161
Dole, Bob, 202
Dunn, Mark, 80, 106, 109, 226

Edens Expressway, 206
Egypt (country), 35, 36, 37, 83
Evanston (town), 23, 24, 26, 39, 57, 75, 116, 120,123, 124, 125, 126, 129, 131, 132, 134, 135, 138, 140, 206
Evanston Hospital, 19, 43

Final Solution, The, 202, 203
Foley, Thomas, 22, 81, 82, 92
Fortmann, Johann N., 20, 57, 58, 59, 60, 61, 65, 90, 95, 167, 199, 201
France (country), 28, 29, 43, 194, 203
Fremont Street, 131
Friedrich, Maria, 209

Galena (town), 57
Gestapo, 165, 170
Gettysburg Address, 120
Glenco (town), 126, 207
Glenview (town), 25, 39, 114, 115, 116, 196, 206
Goebbels, Joseph, 170, 171, 173, 183, 185, 205
Goebbels, Magda, 205, 206
Goering, Hermann, 173
Gold Rush, The, 40
Graf von Galen, Clemens August, 166, 167
Grant, Ulysses S., 75
Great Chicago Fire, 58, 61, 87, 88, 90, 91, 120

Great Depression, 93, 131, 150, 164, 190
Green Bay (old trail), 43
Gross Point (town), 22, 23, 25, 26, 39, 57, 75, 106, 108, 109, 110, 111, 112, 114, 116, 122, 123, 129, 131, 132, 133, 134, 135, 136, 138, 139, 140
Grosse Pointe (territory), 19, 39, 40, 42, 43, 44, 48, 52, 53, 57, 58, 60, 61, 65, 66, 67, 68, 73, 83, 84, 91, 130, 137, 167, 195

Hanisch, Reinhold, 156
Henik, John, 13
Henry, St. (parish), 61, 196, 201
Herod, I, 33, 34, 35, 36
Heskemann, Bernard, 20, 22, 64, 65, 66, 68, 79, 95, 201
Heston, Charlton, 202
Highland Park (town), 207
Hitler, Adolf, 11, 14, 17, 25, 27, 146, 155, 156, 157, 160, 161, 162, 163, 164, 165, 166, 167, 168, 169, 170, 173, 175, 183, 185, 188, 195, 196, 199, 205, 210
Hitler Youth, 163, 164, 165, 166, 169
Hoffmann Letters, The, 47
Holy Name Cathedral, 141

Illinois (state), 39, 42, 43, 57, 81, 83, 138, 176, 208
Illinois Historical Society, 14, 209
Iowa (state), 43
Italy (country), 165

Jacoby, John, 138, 139, 179, 180
Jacoment, J.B.U., 62
Japan (country), 29, 165
Jefferson, Thomas, 119
Jesus Christ, 33-36, 38, 78, 159, 188, 196, 201
John, Saint, 188
John Mick Tavern, 134
Joliet (town), 57
Joseph, of Nazareth/the Worker, 15, 33-38, 83, 84, 196, 201
Joseph, St. (mission), 19, 20, 46, 52, 115
Joseph, St. (parish/church), 11-15, 17, 20, 22-26, 28, 30, 41, 52-55, 57-69, 74, 77, 79-85, 87, 103, 105, 108, 116, 121, 129, 135, 136, 139, 141-143, 146-151, 176, 177, 179, 184, 185, 187-199, 201, 208-211
Joseph, St. (school), 94-99, 109, 121, 135, 138
Judea (region), 33, 34

Kane, Francis, 209
Kartlaub, Peter, 63
Kalvelage, F.L., 90, 139
Kenilworth (town), 39, 126, 138
Kolbe, Maximilian, 204, 205
Kopp, Anthony, 63
Ku Klux Klan (KKK), 131
Kubizek, August, 155
Kuepfer, Lawrence, 62

Lake Michigan, 42, 88, 89, 110
Land Year, The, 169
Las Vegas (city), 131, 140
Lincoln (town), 81
Lincoln, Abraham, 120
Lincoln Park (neighborhood), 88
Lincolnwood (town), 207
Listecki, Jerome, 209

London (city), 67
Loyola University, 112
Luke, Saint, 188, 189

Majdanek (camp), 203, 204
Mallinckrodt (building & park), 24, 97, 108, 112, 113, 202, 208
Mallinckrodt, Pauline von, 112
Matthew, Saint, 34, 35, 36, 188, 189
Matthew, Gospel According to, — see "Matthew, Saint"
Mark, Saint, 188, 189
Mary, of Nazareth, 34, 36, 37, 196
Mary's, St. (parish), 81
Mason, Roswell, 88
McCarthy, Joseph, 187, 188, 189, 208
McCarthy, Smith, and Eggig, 208
McKinley, William, 75
Mein Kampf, 160, 161
Memorial Park Cemetery, 26, 116, 207
Michael, St. (parish), 63, 64
Milwaukee (city), 54, 111
Morton Grove (town), 206
Moselle Valley (region), 39
Moses, 36, 196
Mundelein, George,
Mundelein Seminary – see "St. Mary of the Lake Seminary",
Munich (city), 151, 157, 158
Munich Agreement, 193
Munich Beer Hall Putsch, 161, 175, 210
Münster (city), 59

National Association for the Advancement of Colored People (NAACP), 131
Native American(s), 19, 40, 43, 188, 189
Nazareth (city), 34, 83

—Jesus – see "Jesus Christ"
—Joseph – see "Joseph"
—Mary – see "Mary"
Nazism (National Socialism)
—Ideology, 161-163, 166, 170, 173-176, 195, 196, 199, 202-206
—Political Party, 160-171, 173-176, 182-187, 195, 196, 202-206
Netstraeter, Franz, 19, 78 102, 103, 108, 179
Netstraeter, William
—youth, 19, 78, 183
— education, 21, 78, 79
—as pastor, 22-26, 77, 81-83, 90-101, 135-145, 147-151, 210, 211
—as politician/village president, 2-25, 109, 119-125, 138-140
—real-estate, 105-117
—last will & testament, 26, 28, 149-151, 176-187
New Trier (school), 11, 14, 25, 126, 127, 128
New World, The (newspaper), 101, 102
Neumann, John, 26, 27, 147, 182, 183, 208, 209
Night of the Long Knives, The, 169, 170
Nike (company), 133
Northbrook (town), 39, 206
Northfield (town), 39
Northwestern University, 130, 132

Obama, Barack, 120
Operation: Overlord, 203
Orsenigo, Cesare, 168
Ouilmette, Anton and family, 43, 84
Our Lady of Perpetual Help (parish), 25, 114, 115
Paraoh, 36
Pavone, Frank, 120
Pennsylvania (state), 111
Persia (country), 34

Peter, St. (parish), 21, 68, 97, 116, 129
Pfleger, Michael, 120
Phair, Liz, 202
Pius XII, Pope, 27, 170, 173, 184
Plathe, Gerhard H., 20, 53, 57
Poesch, Anton, 92, 96, 108, 116, 199, 201
Poland (country), 28, 29, 165, 193, 194, 195
Pollard, John E., 11, 12, 213
Pottawatomie (tribe), 19, 43
Prussia (country), 37, 39

Quarter, William, 19, 21, 26, 52, 53, 146
Quigley Seminary, 173

Radio City Music Hall, 189
Reconstruction Era, 66, 67, 82, 120
Redemptorist (religious order), 63, 65
Rhineland (region), 39
Rogers Park (neighborhood), 206
Roosevelt, Franklin D., 27, 175, 208
Roosevelt, Theodore, 75
Rumsfeld, Donald, 202
Rush, Benjamin, 130

School Sisters of St. Francis, 23, 94, 109, 208
Schulte, Maria, 19, 78, 179
Seti I, - see "Pharoh"
Sisters of Christian Charity, 111
Skokie (town), 21, 25, 26, 39, 57, 68, 75, 97, 100, 116, 117, 120, 129, 140, 196, 206, 207
St. Francis de Sales Seminary, 78
Standard Beer, 134
Starr, Merritt, 126
Stauder, Nicholas, 62
Stein, Edith, 204

Stolp, Byron, 126

Trier (city), 19, 39, 40, 81, 177
Trier (school), see "New Trier"
Trump, Donald J., 120
Tschider, 63

USCCB (United States of Catholic Bishops), 120
University of Münster, 78
University of Paderborn, 78
University of St. Mary of the Lake, 21, 26, 146, 147, 150, 176, 182, 187, 194, 208

Van de Velde, James O., 20, 61
Vatican, The, 28, 167, 174, 184
Vienna (city), 25, 155, 157

Wandering Church, 169
Wilmette
—Town/Village Government, 11, 12, 22, 23, 59, 75, 77, 79, 84, 85, 87, 90, 100, 104-108, 110, 112-115, 117, 120- 126, 129, 131, 123, 138-140, 149, 177, 179, 187, 193-195, 202
—Park District, 112, 202
Wilmette Citizen's Club, 124
Wilmette Life (newspaper), 149, 223
Winnetka (town), 39, 75, 126, 129, 132, 206
With Burning Concern, 170, 171
Wilson, A.N., 161, 162
Wilson, Rainn, 202
Wisconsin (state), 21, 40, 43, 54, 62, 83
Women's Christian Temperance Union, 130, 132, 135,137
World War I, 146, 157, 160, 163, 178

World War II, 16, 28, 30, 165, 194, 195, 199, 203, 206

Zwick, Edward, 202

About the Authors

Daniel Jolls holds a B.A. in English from the University of Illinois at Chicago (UIC). He served as the president of the Newman Catholic Student Organization at UIC's St. John Paul II Newman Center from 2017 to 2018. In this role, he orchestrated over 50 campus outreach events. In 2017, he wrote and presented a senior honors thesis entitled, "Mental Health in Cinema: A Spectatorship and Allegiance Approach," identifying and analyzing the positive trends in how mentally ill individuals are represented in film. He reworked this thesis to specifically highlight mentally ill youth for a presentation at the UNIV Congress in Rome, Italy in the spring of 2018.

Michael Jolls is the author of the books *The Films of Steven Spielberg* (2018) and *Make Hollywood Great Again: Cinema in the Era of President Trump* (2020). He was also assistant editor on the book *David Fincher: Interviews* (2014). Jolls has also produced over a hundred various film projects. His works include *6 Rules* (2011); the *Uncle Colt & Cletus* series (2012-2014); *Cathedral of the North Shore* (2013); *The Great Chicago Filmmaker* (2015); the *#SelfieGuy* series (2015-2017); *Sell Me This Pen* (2018) and *A Sad State of Affairs* (2020).

Made in the USA
Coppell, TX
01 December 2020